Devolution to Scotland:
The Legal Aspects

Devolution to Scotland: The Legal Aspects

Contemplating the Imponderable

Edited by

T StJ N Bates

Centre for Parliamentary and Legislative Studies
University of Strathclyde

T&T CLARK
EDINBURGH
1997

T&T CLARK LTD
59 GEORGE STREET
EDINBURGH EH2 2LQ
SCOTLAND

First published 1997

ISBN 0 567 00529 1

British Library Cataloguing-in-Publication Data
A catalogue record for this book is available from the British Library

Typeset by Fakenham Photosetting Limited, Fakenham, Norfolk
Printed and bound in Scotland by Bell & Bain Ltd, Glasgow

Contents

Introduction

After some twenty years, devolution to Scotland again seems destined to become a matter of major parliamentary concern. For some this may appear as yet another turn of the political wheel of fortune. Indeed, the old and jaded might look back to the 1970s, reflect on the devolution legislation of the time as rather less than satisfactory and distinctly unimaginative, and sigh. The even older and perhaps more jaded might cast their minds back not only to the 1970s but to previous times when the politics and populace, both in Scotland and in the United Kingdom as a whole, demonstrated their resistance to constitutional innovation, and sigh more deeply. Yet time has moved on and the continuing asset of the contemporary is that it brings with it new enthusiasms and fresh ideas to address changing circumstances.

Circumstances *have* changed. We are no longer a neophyte member state of the European Communities beginning to come to terms with constitutional, economic and political implications of membership but a state, however reluctantly, responding in a more sophisticated manner to our integration in an enlarged and enlarging European Union, which is itself in the throes of significant institutional change. We live in a state which has experienced profound change in its economic structure and objectives. It is a state in which there has been a significant shift in visible trade from manufacture to services and where, in any event, the microchip has displaced the oil rig as the focus of economic endeavour. It is a state in which there has been an apparently irreversible shift to privatisation and regulation. It is a state which has been subjected to successive reorganisation of local government and a profound decline in its role. Perhaps as a response, it is a state which has witnessed an increasing preoccupation with administrative law, in particular – following procedural reforms which have enhanced its availability – with judicial review and the use which may be made of it.

In tandem with such structural change there has been an attitudinal change. There is a marked increase in public and political willingness to re-evaluate constitutional tenets and institutions: the desirability of a written constitution and of a bill of rights, the role and working of the monarchy, of Parliament, of central and local government. Legislative and executive devolution no longer stand alone, perhaps with electoral reform, as constitutional issues which fall to be addressed from time to time. It may be that this is one reason why debate in Scotland on devolution now appears more self-confident and less strident. On the other hand, it is as yet unclear whether this more general evaluation of the constitution will assist or inhibit a rapid and positive outcome for the contemporary proposals for Scottish devolution.

The political circumstances in which these proposals are being developed have changed. In the 1970s they were developed by a somewhat precarious coalition Government anxious to retain office; in the 1990s they are being developed by a party in opposition, confident of taking office, as part of an ambitious programme of constitutional reform and following extensive public collaborative efforts with Scottish interests, and with a consequential degree of rapprochement with some other parties. As a result, whereas the devolution proposals of the 1970s were largely developed in Whitehall and an attempt was then made to convince Scotland, and the rest of the United Kingdom, of their efficacy and coherence, on this occasion the general structure of the devolution proposals has been developed in public deliberation in Scotland, in particular by the Scottish Constitutional Convention and, subject to the result of the 1997 General Election, we will await the Whitehall response. However, although there has been Scottish political and institutional involvement in the development of the devolution proposals and significant politico-legal comment on them outwith the jurisdiction, at this point there has been relatively little Scottish legal comment on the proposals. It was that lack which eventually led to this small collection of papers.

In 1993 the University of Strathclyde established a Centre for Parliamentary and Legislative Studies to stimulate teaching and research on the drafting and interpretation of legislation. In passing it may be noted that this enlightened decision was itself perhaps a reflection of other changing circumstances, namely a greater appreciation in legal education of the importance of legislation as a source of law and of the need for the lawyer to be more fully trained in its use. It was under the auspices of the Centre that an invitation was extended in April 1996 to a small group of Scottish academic and practising lawyers to discuss some of the implications of the contemporary devolution proposals at a series of evening meetings at the University. The membership of the group has been fluid, but the authors of the papers, together with Professor Ian Willock of the University of Dundee, have been the regular members. Members prepared papers which were revised following always penetrating and often vigorous discussion, although as presented here they still represent the views of the authors rather than of the group as a whole.

It was not our initial intention to publish the papers. Indeed we may be criticised as somewhat self-indulgent and foolhardy for doing so. Self-indulgent in that our discussions have focused on some of the issues only; but, in the contemporary circumstances, these were the issues which we felt were either in themselves novel or which had acquired a novel dimension. Foolhardy in that despite the continuing work of the Scottish Constitutional Convention and others, substantial elements of the devolution proposals await refinement, and in many instances meaningful professional comment will not be possible until a bill is published. Nevertheless, we considered that it was opportune to offer some Scottish apolitical commentary on the proposals as they exist. It was, we felt, better to contribute to the preparation of the menu rather than simply await a later opportunity to comment on the meal. The group will however stay in being with the intention of monitoring the devolution proposals as they are further developed.

I end with my personal thanks to the members of the group, and in particular my fellow authors, for taking the time from their busy professional lives to discuss and write on the devolution proposals to date; to Professor Alan Paterson, for encouraging and facilitating our meetings; and to our publishers for undertaking to publish, and publish so promptly, our deliberations.

St John Bates
February 1997

Strategies for the Future: A Lasting Parliament for Scotland?

Jean McFadden and William Bain

Introduction

The difficult issues in attempting to achieve legislative devolution for Scotland within the United Kingdom are well known: the 'West Lothian' question; Scottish representation at Westminster; the future of the office of Secretary of State for Scotland; taxation powers. There is yet another: whether or not to attempt to 'entrench'[1] all or part of a future Scotland Act – that is, whether or not it is possible for the Act of Parliament establishing a Scottish Parliament to be protected in such a way as to prevent its repeal by a subsequent Act of the United Kingdom Parliament passed by a simple majority in the Lords and the Commons and given the Royal Assent. Is such a scheme practical or possible under our present constitutional arrangements, or should other methods to promote moral or political entrenchment of the Scotland Act be sought?

Parliamentary sovereignty and entrenchment

The seemingly immoveable obstacle to a legislative entrenchment mechanism is the doctrine of the sovereignty of the United Kingdom Parliament, described by its most prominent proponent, A. V. Dicey, as 'the dominant characteristic of our political institutions'[2] and 'the very keystone' of constitutional law in this country. Parliament, for this purpose, means the Queen, the House of Lords and the House of Commons acting together. Dicey defined the principle as follows:

> 'The principle of Parliamentary sovereignty means neither more nor less than this, namely, that Parliament thus defined has, under the English constitution, the right to make or unmake any law whatever; and further, that no person or body is recognised

[1] As is the practice with regional government elsewhere in Europe – see, eg, Title VIII, Chapter III of the Spanish Constitution (1978) and art 79 of the German Basic Law (1949) – and in certain Commonwealth countries – see, eg, Australian Constitution, s 128.

[2] *An Introduction to the Study of the Law of the Constitution* (10th edn), p 39.

by the law of England as having a right to override or set aside the legislation of Parliament.'[3]

The traditional doctrine breaks down into three basic tenets:

(i)   that no Parliament may bind its successors as to the form or content of subsequent legislation;
(ii) that no Act of Parliament may be held invalid by a United Kingdom court of law; and
(iii) that there is no distinction in terms of procedure between ordinary statutes and those of constitutional significance.

An Act of Parliament may expressly repeal an earlier Act or any part of it. If an Act is passed which conflicts with an earlier Act but does not expressly repeal it, the later Act is taken to repeal the inconsistencies of the earlier Act. The Acquisition of Land (Assessment of Compensation) Act 1919 provided that 'so far as inconsistent with this Act [other statutory] provisions ... shall not have effect'.[4] The Housing Act 1925 altered the 1919 rules of compensation. In *Vauxhall Estates Ltd* v *Liverpool Corporation*[5] the court rejected the argument that the 1919 Act had bound future Parliaments to the extent that they could not legislate inconsistently with the 1919 Act except by words of express repeal. In another case on the same subsection, *Ellen Street Estates Ltd* v *Minister of Health*,[6] Maugham LJ said:

> 'The Legislature cannot, according to our constitution, bind itself as to the form of subsequent legislation, and it is impossible for Parliament to enact that in a subsequent statute, dealing with the same subject-matter, there can be no implied repeal.'[7]

These two cases, which concern the doctrine of implied repeal, have been used to support a broader argument, that Parliament may never bind its successors.[8]

It is well established that no court in the United Kingdom can hold an Act of Parliament invalid. As Lord Dunedin said in *Mortensen* v *Peters*:[9] 'For us, an Act of Parliament, duly passed by Lords, Commons and assented to by the King is supreme and we are bound to give effect to its terms.' In this case United Kingdom law was inconsistent with international law. Similarly, where a

---

[3] Dicey at pp 39–40. For our purposes, we assume that 'English' and 'England' are simply careless synonyms for 'British' and 'the United Kingdom' and not the result of a calculated omission – perhaps a controversial assumption none the less.
[4] Section 7(1).
[5] [1932] 1 KB 733.
[6] [1934] 1 KB 590.
[7] Ibid at p 597.
[8] See H. W. R. Wade, 'The Basis of Legal Sovereignty' [1955] CLJ 172.
[9] (1906) 8 F (J) 93 at p 100.

United Kingdom statute conflicts with a treaty, the United Kingdom courts will not hold the United Kingdom statute invalid, as 'what that statute itself enacts cannot be unlawful, because what the statute says and provides is itself the law and the highest form of law that is known to this country'.[10] Nor will the courts inquire into the proceedings on a bill in its passage through Parliament, provided that the Act has been passed by the Lords and Commons and has received the Royal Assent.[11]

Statutes of constitutional significance such as the European Communities Act 1972 are enacted in exactly the same way as any other primary legislation, although there is a parliamentary convention that bills of prime constitutional importance should have the committee stage taken in a Committee of the Whole House.

Thus the traditional view of parliamentary sovereignty allows no legal limitation on that sovereignty. Traditionalists are however forced to concede that there may be practical limitations.[12] For example, the Anglo-German Agreement Act 1890 which ceded Heligoland to Germany was repealed by the Statute Law Revision Act 1953, but not even the most ardent adherent of Dicey expects the United Kingdom to attempt to recover Heligoland. Similarly, the effects of Acts conferring independence on Britain's former colonies cannot be undone, even though it is theoretically possible, but politically unlikely, for Parliament to pass repealing Acts. In any event, although a United Kingdom court would give effect to such a repealing statute enacted by Westminster, it is highly unlikely that the courts in the former colony would do so.[13] As Stratford ACJ said in *Ndlwana* v *Hofmeyr*:[14] 'Freedom once conferred cannot be revoked.'

According to the traditional view, a Scotland Act establishing a devolved Scottish Parliament (as opposed to an independent Scottish Parliament) could simply be repealed by a subsequent Act of the Westminster Parliament, passed by a simple majority, just as the Northern Ireland Constitution Act 1973[15] repealed the provisions of the Government of Ireland Act 1920 which had

---

[10] *Cheney* v *Conn* [1968] 1 All ER 779, per Ungoed Thomas J at p 782.

[11] *Pickin* v *British Railways Board* [1974] AC 765. See also *Sillars* v *Smith* 1982 SLT (Notes) 539 in a specifically Scottish context.

[12] Dicey believed in practical rather than legal limits on the exercise of the power of government, and he advocated the use of the referendum as the exercise of a check on government by the people, though this seemed to be motivated by his opposition to Irish Home Rule, which he suspected was shared by the British people. For a fascinating account of his less well-known writings, see V. Bogdanor, *Politics and the Constitution* (1995), Introduction, and C. Munro, *Studies in Constitutional Law*, ch 5, who draws the distinction between legal and practical limitations on parliamentary sovereignty.

[13] See *Madzimbamuto* v *Lardner-Burke* [1969] 1 AC 645, per Lord Reid at p 723.

[14] [1937] AD 229 at p 237.

[15] Section 31.

established the Northern Ireland Parliament at Stormont. To the traditional-ists, it would make no difference even if the Act establishing a Scottish Parliament contained a provision that the Parliament should not be abolished except with, say, the consent of the Scottish people expressed in a referendum, or by a two-thirds' majority in the House of Commons.

There is, however, a revisionist view of parliamentary sovereignty which questions whether the doctrine is as absolute as the traditionalists suppose. The earliest proponent was probably Sir Ivor Jennings,[16] followed by R. V. F. Heuston[17] and J. D. B. Mitchell.[18] Although they do not question the proposition that no Act of Parliament can be protected absolutely from subsequent amendment or repeal, they argue that it might be possible for a Parliament to bind its successors as to the 'manner and form'[19] of subsequent enactments. If the Scotland Act contained a provision such as described above, that a Scottish Parliament should not be abolished unless supported by, say, the Scottish people in a referendum or an enhanced majority in the House of Commons (which would ensure that it had cross-party support), the manner-and-form school argue that a successor Parliament would be bound by the provision. They support this position by reference to a number of Com-monwealth cases.

In *Attorney-General for New South Wales* v *Trethowan*[20] the Judicial Committee of the Privy Council upheld the grant of an injunction restraining the presentation to the Governor-General for the Royal Assent of a Bill to abolish the Second Chamber of the New South Wales legislature because there had been no compliance with an earlier Act which required such a proposal to be passed in a referendum.[21]

The South African case of *Harris* v *Minister of the Interior*[22] concerned the validity of an Act which was passed in the ordinary way, but which, it was argued, was not valid because it concerned a proposal relating to the franchise which required to be passed by a two-thirds' majority of both Houses sitting together. The Appellate Division of the Supreme Court of South Africa upheld the entrenching provisions of the earlier Act and declared the later Act invalid.

In *Bribery Commissioner* v *Ranasinghe*[23] the case turned on the Ceylon

---

[16] Jennings, *The Law and the Constitution* (2nd edn).

[17] R. V. F. Heuston, *Essays in Constitutional Law* (2nd edn).

[18] J. D. B. Mitchell, *Constitutional Law* (2nd edn, 1968).

[19] The phrase 'manner and form' is taken from the Colonial Laws Validity Act 1865, s 5.

[20] [1932] AC 526.

[21] Although Dixon CJ seems to have changed his mind on whether the courts ought to interfere in these circumstances: *Hughes and Vale* v *Gair* (1954) 90 CLR 203.

[22] [1952] 2 SALR (AD) 428.

[23] [1965] AC 172.

Constitution Order (1946) which contained a provision that no bill to amend or repeal the Order should be presented for the Royal Assent unless it had endorsed on it a certificate of the Speaker to the effect that not less than two-thirds of the House of Representatives had voted in favour of the bill. The Judicial Committee of the Privy Council held that a later Act, which contained a provision in conflict with the 1946 Order, and whose bill did not contain the requisite Speaker's Certificate, was void.

The manner-and-form school argue that the courts could take a similar view of an Act of the United Kingdom Parliament which had not followed the procedure laid down in an earlier Act. The argument takes two forms. First, although any Act of Parliament can amend or repeal an earlier Act, the courts have to be satisfied that the later Act is in fact an Act. If Parliament has laid down a special procedure for the passing of certain Acts and that procedure is not followed, the courts may be disposed to hold the measure invalid because it is not an *Act*, just as they can hold subordinate legislation to be invalid. The second form of the argument is that Parliament can redefine itself for certain purposes. So, Parliament for most purposes consists of the Queen, the Lords and Commons, but under the Parliament Acts, 1911 and 1949, it is redefined in certain circumstances as the Queen and the Commons only. Cannot Parliament be redefined by adding another element – for example, the people consulted in a referendum or a special majority of the House of Commons? It is argued, particularly since the decision in *R* v *Secretary of State for Transport, ex parte Factortame Ltd*,[24] that our membership of the European Union has already added another element to the definition of Parliament in certain circumstances, and altered our idea of traditional parliamentary sovereignty.

The traditionalists reject the manner-and-form arguments. The Commonwealth cases are dismissed as no authority for the proposition that a manner or form requirement for United Kingdom Acts of Parliament would be held binding by United Kingdom courts, the distinction being that, unlike the United Kingdom Parliament, the Commonwealth legislatures derived their power to legislate from a written instrument which laid down the procedural requirement. Also rejected is the argument that an 'Act' or 'Parliament' can be

[24] [1991] 1 AC 603. See also H. W. R. Wade, 'What has happened to the Sovereignty of Parliament?' (1991) 107 LQR 1 and 'Sovereignty – Revolution or Evolution?' (1996) 112 LQR 568, who now accepts that Parliament in 1972 bound its successors to enshrining the supremacy of European law in UK law, as required by the Treaty of Rome, and A. Bradley, 'The Sovereignty of Parliament – in Perpetuity', in J. Jowell and D. Oliver (eds), *The Changing Constitution* (3rd edn, 1994). De Smith (7th edn), p 89, argues that Parliament is bound, unless and until the UK decides to withdraw from the European Union entirely. Some commentators suggest that the supremacy of EU law restores the actual concept of sovereignty, as intended at the time of the 1688 revolution: see I. Loveland, 'Parliamentary Sovereignty and the European Community' (1996) Parl Aff 517 at p 534.

redefined. This leads some traditionalists to maintain that Acts passed under
the Parliament Acts, 1911 and 1949, are not Acts at all but a special type of
subordinate legislation.[25]

Nevertheless, there have been occasions when the United Kingdom Parliament has attempted to bind its successors. Let us leave aside for the moment
the question as to whether the Acts of Union 1706–07 contain provisions which
are fundamental and unalterable.[26] In this century, Parliament has passed
legislation which purports to bind its successors. The Statute of Westminster
1931, which provided for the legislative independence of the Dominions
contains, in s 4, the provision that no Act of the Parliament of the United
Kingdom passed after the commencement of the Statute of Westminster
should extend to a Dominion unless it is expressly declared in the subsequent
Act that the Dominion had requested and consented to the enactment. Various
Acts conferring independence on former colonies contain provisions whereby
the United Kingdom Parliament purports to renounce its power to legislate for
them, and the Canada Act 1982 provided that 'No Act of the Parliament of the
United Kingdom passed after the Constitution Act 1982 comes into force shall
extend to Canada as part of its law'.[27]

The European Communities Act 1972, s 2(4), provides, *inter alia*, that 'any
enactment passed or to be passed . . . shall be construed and have effect subject
to the foregoing provisions of this section'. This purports to secure that even
future Acts of the United Kingdom Parliament must yield to directly applicable
European Union law. The decision in *Factortame*[28] emphasises the supremacy
of European Union law, as long as the United Kingdom remains a member
state of the Union. The Northern Ireland Constitution Act 1973, s 1, provides
that Northern Ireland shall not cease to be part of the United Kingdom without
the consent of the majority of the people in Northern Ireland voting in a
referendum. The Scotland Act 1978, s 85, required the Secretary of State for
Scotland to lay before Parliament a draft Order in Council for the repeal of the
1978 Act if it appeared to him that less than 40 per cent of the persons entitled
to vote in a referendum had voted 'Yes' on the question 'Do you want the
provisions of the Scotland Act 1978 to be put into effect?' So there is precedent
for Parliament enacting provisions which seek to bind future Parliaments. But
the question as to what authority can require a future Parliament to comply
remains untested. Let us take the Northern Ireland Constitution Act 1973,

---

[25] Wade, note 24 above, p 265; O. Hood Phillips, *Constitutional and Administrative Law* (7th edn,
1987), p 90.
[26] See T. B. Smith, *The Laws of Scotland: Stair Memorial Encyclopaedia*, Vol 5; J. D. B. Mitchell,
note 18 above.
[27] Section 2.
[28] *R v Secretary of State for Transport, ex parte Factortame Ltd (No 2)* [1991] 1 AC 603.

which is probably the closest parallel to an 'entrenched' Scotland Act. Would the courts in Northern Ireland or in Britain assume jurisdiction? If so, would they be prepared to hold that a subsequent Parliament has lost the right to repeal the 1973 Act either expressly or by implication? Questions of *locus standi* and of effective relief also arise. 'To put the matter another way, it is of little avail to ask if the Parliament of Great Britain "can" do this thing or that without going on to enquire who can stop them if they do.'[29]

Scotland – parliamentary or popular sovereignty?

In pre-Union Scotland, sovereignty was not said to reside with the King or with the Scottish Parliament. The monarch was not above the law, and in respect of 'unconstitutional' actings, was controlled (by threats of force if necessary) by the Estates of the Parliament or groups of the subjects. Governmental power was shared between a variety of institutions – the Church and the Convention of Royal Burghs – and not vested in Parliament alone. The populace could be said to have had a limited legislative competence in that legislation could be set aside through the operation of the doctrine of desuetude; where a custom had been established contrary to the provisions of a statute, which demonstrated the will of the people no longer to be bound by that statute, and that it was effectively repealed.[30] The historical distinction between the powers of the pre-Union Scottish and English Parliaments was put by Dicey and Rait:

> '[T]he Parliament of Scotland never had, or felt that it had, the omnipotence of the English Parliament. Indeed the Scottish Parliament almost at all times acknowledged some power which restrained or competed with parliamentary authority.'[31]

The Acts of Union, in both jurisdictions, had nothing to say on the vexed question of sovereignty. Only when the litigation as to whether our present monarch could be styled Elizabeth II was brought in the early 1950s was this issue to achieve prominence again. Lord President Cooper's famous, though *obiter*, remarks in *MacCormick v Lord Advocate*[32] on sovereignty and the Union have formed the foundation of any challenge to the notion of the absolute sovereignty of the United Kingdom Parliament in a Scottish context. He said:

> 'The principle of the unlimited sovereignty of Parliament is a distinctively English principle which has no counterpart in Scottish constitutional law. ... I have difficulty

---

[29] *MacCormick v Lord Advocate* 1953 SC 396, per Lord President Cooper at p 411. See also N. MacCormick, 'Does the United Kingdom have a Constitution? Reflections on *MacCormick v Lord Advocate*' [1978] NILQ 1.

[30] See T. B. Smith, *A Short Commentary on the Law of Scotland*, ch 3.

[31] A. V. Dicey and R. S. Rait, *Thoughts on the Union between England and Scotland* (1920), p 21.

[32] 1953 SC 396.

in seeing why it should have been supposed that the new Parliament of Great Britain must inherit all the peculiar characteristics of the English Parliament but none of the Scottish Parliament, as if all that happened in 1707 was that Scottish representatives were admitted to the Parliament of England. That is not what was done.'[33]

He quoted Dicey and Rait to emphasise the point:

'A sovereign Parliament, in short, though it cannot be logically bound to abstain from changing any given law, may, by the fact that an Act when it was passed had been declared to be unchangeable, receive a warning that it cannot be changed without grave danger to the Constitution of the country.'[34]

But no mechanism for enforcing the Act of Union against subsequent contrary legislation of the United Kingdom Parliament was proposed, nor were the circumstances in which it might be appropriate to do so outlined. Lord Cooper, however, reserved his opinion[35] with regard to the provisions of art XIX, which secures the continuance of the Court of Session and the High Court of Justiciary, and art XVIII, which concerns 'private right'.

The reluctance of the Scottish courts to become embroiled in a full-scale constitutional tug-of-war with Parliament has been clear, despite restating that certain articles of the Treaty of Union may be justiciable. In *Gibson* v *Lord Advocate*[36] Lord Keith was clear that it was not the function of the courts to inquire into 'the utility of certain legislative measures as regards the population generally',[37] but reserved his opinion as to what the position would be if the United Kingdom Parliament passed an Act purporting to abolish the Court of Session or the Church of Scotland, or to substitute English law for the entire body of Scots private law.

In *Stewart* v *Henry*[38] three individuals claimed that the Abolition of Domestic Rates etc (Scotland) Act 1987 was unconstitutional since it contravened, *inter alia*, art XVIII. They claimed that as the community charge was a tax imposed on Scotland only at that time, it affected a matter of private right, and was not for the evident utility of the subjects in Scotland, and even if the legislation affected public right instead, it could not be valid as it did not make the law the same throughout the United Kingdom. Sheriff Stewart quoted Lord Keith, Lord President Cooper and J. D. B. Mitchell, and while holding that a summary application was an inappropriate way in which to raise these matters, maintained there was no absolute bar to consideration of 'evident utility' in the courts.[39]

---

[33] Ibid at p 411.
[34] Ibid at p 412; Dicey and Rait, note 31 above, pp 252–253.
[35] Ibid at p 412.
[36] 1975 SC 136.
[37] Ibid at p 144.
[38] 1989 SLT (Sh Ct) 34.
[39] Ibid at p 38 L.

In *Pringle, Petitioner*,[40] Pringle applied to the *nobile officium* of the Court of Session seeking an order that he was not required to pay the community charge for 1989–90 on the basis that the charge was in breach of art IV of the Act of Union in that those resident in England in that year enjoyed the 'right, privilege and advantage' of not being required to pay the community charge. In dismissing the petition Lord President Hope reserved his opinion as to whether art IV has the effect for the future that it would be a breach of that article for Parliament to legislate

> 'in such a way that the subjects of one part of the United Kingdom enjoyed rights, privileges and advantages in regard to the immunity from methods of taxation which were not already in force in 1707 without similar rights, privileges and advantages being communicated to those resident in the other part'.[41]

Lord Weir also expressly reserved his opinion on the purpose and effect of art IV.

So far there has been no decision where the courts have held that the Acts of Union restrict the legislative competence of Parliament.[42] However, the positions of the Church of Scotland and of the Court of Session, to which Lord Keith referred in *Gibson* are worth noting. The Protestant Religion and Presbyterian Church Act 1706 declared that 'the said true Presbyterian Religion [was] to continue without any alteration to the people in this land in all succeeding generations'. This Act was incorporated into the Act of Union (art XXV) and was declared to be a fundamental and essential condition of the Union in all time coming.

The Church of Scotland Act 1921 enacted as lawful the 'Articles Declaratory of the Constitution of the Church of Scotland in Matters Spiritual' and appears, *inter alia*, to attempt to entrench them in respect of existing legislation by providing 'that in all questions of construction, the Declaratory Articles shall prevail and that all such statutes and laws [affecting the Church of Scotland in matters spiritual at present in force] shall be construed in conformity therewith and in subordination thereto'.[43]

In *Ballantyne* v *Presbytery of Wigtown*[44] the Lord Justice-Clerk, Lord Aitchison, declared that s 1 was a clear and unambiguous affirmation of the supremacy of the articles in every conflict with existing laws or statutes touching the matters with which they deal. If a matter falls within those defined in the 1921 Act as 'matters spiritual', it is solely within the jurisdiction

---

[40] 1991 SLT 330.

[41] Ibid at p 333 D. See further D. Edwards, 'The Treaty of Union: more hints of constitutionalism' (1992) 12 *Legal Studies* 34.

[42] See Bogdanor, note 12 above, p 4.

[43] Section 1.

[44] 1936 SC 625.

of the ecclesiastical courts and 'the matter is at an end, and neither the statute nor the common law nor previous judicial decision, whether upon statute or upon common law, can avail to bring the matter within the jurisdiction of the civil authority'.[45] Most ministers and members of the Church of Scotland certainly believe that the 1921 Act confers on the Church doctrinal independence from the state and that s 1 of the Act is an entrenching provision.

Article XIX of the Act of Union provides 'that the Court of Session or College of Justice do after the Union ... remain in all time coming within Scotland'. A number of proposals to reform the Court of Session between 1785 and 1830 were strongly resisted on constitutional grounds. A proposal was made in 1872 to abolish the appellate jurisdiction of the House of Lords and the Privy Council and replace them with an Imperial Court of Appeal. Lord Cairns objected that this was precluded because

> 'by our Treaty of Union with Scotland we expressly contracted that under no circumstances were appeals from the Scotch Courts to be sent to any of the courts in Westminster Hall'.[46]

The Government accepted that position and the bill which was subsequently introduced in the House gave the new Court of Appeal no jurisdiction over Scottish, or Irish, appeals.[47] Was it an acceptance of statutory entrenchment or concern over the political implications of the provision which caused the Government of the day to draw back?

The Scottish Constitutional Convention and entrenchment

From the start the Scottish Constitutional Convention was hostile to the notion that parliamentary sovereignty – which it termed 'a constitutional fiction which cloaks the effective exercise of sovereign power by the governing political party'[48] – applied to the governance of Scotland. The risk of repeal or substantial amendment of the Scotland Act under such a system was recognised, and popular sovereignty[49] was adopted as 'the fundamental tenet of ... faith'.[50] It reiterated the view that the pre-Union Scottish Parliament had never been sovereign, and that the power of the monarch, acting through Parliament, had been constrained by the Church, the nobility and landowners who could

---

[45] 1936 SC 625 at 654.

[46] 210 HL Debs, col 1990 (30th April 1872).

[47] The bill was the Supreme Court of Judicature Bill. See also A. J. MacLean, 'The 1707 Union: Scots Law and the House of Lords' (1983) 4 JLH 50; ibid. 'The House of Lords and Appeals from the High Court of Justiciary, 1707–1887' 1985 JR 192.

[48] Towards a Scottish Parliament (Scottish Constitutional Convention, 1989) p 16.

[49] See, eg, T. B. Smith, *A Short Commentary on the Law of Scotland*, p 57, who refers to Scottish sovereignty residing in the community.

[50] Towards a Scottish Parliament, note 47 above, at p 17.

'legitimately claim to represent a considerable part of the population'.[51] Although the Scottish Parliament had been abolished, the sovereignty of the Scottish people had not.

The Convention sought to give practical effect to this theory of Scottish sovereignty by acknowledging in its founding Declaration[52] 'the sovereign right of the Scottish people to determine the form of government best suited to their needs'. Three possible forms of procedures were suggested to entrench the Scotland Act:

(i)   parliamentary (involving perhaps a two-thirds' majority of one House or even both);

(ii)   a referendum; or

(iii)   a combination of the preceding two.

It was left for the Convention to determine later which features of a new Scottish constitutional settlement should be unalterable,[53] but a draft entrenchment clause was included in Appendix 1 of *Towards a Scottish Parliament*.[54]

'1 (1)   The enactments described in Schedule 1 to this Act shall not be capable of amendment.

(2)   Amendments to the enactments described in Schedule 2 to this Act may be proposed by the Parliament of Scotland or of the United Kingdom or by a constitutional petition.

(3)   Subject to sub-section (8) below an amendment proposed by either of the aforesaid Parliaments shall be approved in both Parliaments by a majority of all the members who vote.

(4)   A constitutional petition shall be submitted to the Speaker of the aforesaid Parliament and shall contain the full text of the amendment proposed and be signed by parliamentary electors equal in number to at least 15% of the total electorate of the Parliament to which the petition is submitted.

(5)   An amendment proposed by petition shall be submitted for adoption in the same manner as an amendment proposed by the aforesaid Parliament and shall be approved by a majority of all the members who vote.

(6)   An amendment which has been approved as aforesaid shall not take effect unless it is submitted to Scottish parliamentary electors at a referendum held in accordance with Schedule 3 to this Act on a date at least 6 months and not more than 2 years after it has been so approved and is agreed to by a majority of the votes cast.

(7)   An amendment proposed by constitutional petition which fails to obtain the approval of Parliament but which is supported by 40% or more of those members who voted shall take effect if it is submitted to Scottish parliamentary electors at a referendum held in accordance with Schedule 3 to this Act on a date at least 6 months and not more than 2 years after the date on which it fails to obtain approval as aforesaid and is agreed to by a majority of the votes cast.

(8)   An amendment which primarily affects the powers, rights and privileges of the

---

[51]   Ibid.
[52]   Adopted on 30th March 1989.
[53]   *Towards a Scottish Parliament*, note 47 above, at p 21.
[54]   Ibid at p 51.

government of Scotland and does not derogate from the powers, rights and privileges of the government of the United Kingdom shall not require the approval of the Parliament of the United Kingdom.'

The Convention, in a later report, Towards Scotland's Parliament, made clear its intention to make practically and politically impossible any moves by the United Kingdom Parliament to repeal or substantially amend the Scotland Act. The commitment and the challenge to the traditional doctrine of parliamentary sovereignty were clear:

'The Convention is adamant that the powers of the Scottish Parliament, once established, must be entrenched so that they cannot be altered without the consent of the Scottish people. . . . The Act establishing the Scottish Parliament would state that the powers would not be altered without the consent of the Scottish Parliament.'[55]

The Convention, however, recognised that repeal or amendment by Westminster without reference to a Scottish Parliament was constitutionally possible, but its objective was to make that practically and politically impossible.

Following the 1992 General Election, the Scottish Constitutional Convention set up a Constitutional Commission, an independent body, whose remit was to consider and make recommendations on, *inter alia*, the constitutional implications at United Kingdom level of the establishment of a Scottish Parliament, including entrenchment. The Commission concluded that legal entrenchment was not possible, but it recommended that the Convention should seek 'the maximum moral and political entrenchment of the existence and powers of a Scottish Parliament and Executive'[56] by advocating provisions in the Scotland Act which stated the intention of Parliament not to amend the Scotland Act without the consent of the Scottish Parliament, nor to repeal or amend the Scotland Act in such a way as to threaten the Scottish Parliament's existence, without the consent of the Scottish Parliament and the Scottish people directly consulted through a general election or a referendum. It was, however, recognised that such provisions themselves could of course be amended or repealed, so this could only illustrate the opinion of *that particular United Kingdom Parliament at the time of the passing of the Scotland Act*. Implicit in this was the recognition that future United Kingdom Parliaments could not be so bound, but the provisions would at least enshrine the commitment of the Parliament which passed the Act to the principle that these democratic institutions of government should not be unilaterally abolished by the body which established them.

In 1995 the Executive Committee of the Scottish Constitutional Convention

---

[55] Towards Scotland's Parliament (Scottish Constitutional Convention, 1990), p 8.
[56] Further Steps Towards a Scheme for Scotland's Parliament (Scottish Constitutional Commission, 1994), pp 29–30.

considered again the possibility of recommending that an attempt should be made to write entrenching provisions into a future Scotland Act, but was dissuaded by the arguments of Mr George Robertson MP, the Labour Shadow Secretary of State for Scotland. It was still adamant that the powers of the Scottish Parliament should not be altered without the consent of the Scottish Parliament representing the people of Scotland.[57] Despite the view of the Constitutional Commission, it was firmly of the view that the Scotland Act would establish a Parliament with legitimate authority and that the Act's repeal or amendment should be made practically and politically impossible by widespread national and international recognition of that authority. It pointed to examples where entrenchment had been effectively achieved, whatever the constitutional lawyers might say – the status of the Church of Scotland and the primacy of European Union law over domestic law. The Convention opted for a Declaration of the Parliament of the United Kingdom of Great Britain and Northern Ireland, in advance of the Scotland Bill being placed before Parliament, stating that the Act establishing the Scottish Parliament should not be repealed or amended in such a way as to threaten its existence, without the consent of the Scottish people, directly consulted through general election or referendum.[58]

The very formality of the commitment, the Scottish Constitutional Convention argued, would be a significant and visible reminder of the special nature of the institution which had been created.[59] It would be reinforced by the increasing importance of European constitutional structures relating to regional and local government in the member states.

The arguments put forward by Mr Robertson revolved more around practicalities than constitutional theory. The Labour Party has promised to legislate for a Scottish Parliament in its first year in office, following the holding of a pre-legislative referendum in Scotland on the principle of the Scottish Parliament, and on its proposed taxation powers.[60] As stated earlier, the parliamentary convention is that the Committee Stage of bills of great constitutional significance would ordinarily be taken in a Committee of the Whole House.[61] Even if this convention were to be modified as part of the proposed comprehensive review of parliamentary procedure, and the Committee Stage of the Scotland Bill was taken in Standing Committee rather than on the floor of the House, a new Labour Government would be hard pressed to

---

[57] Key Proposals for Scotland's Parliament (1995), p 7.
[58] Scotland's Parliament, Scotland's Right (Scottish Constitutional Convention, 1995), p 7.
[59] Ibid, at p 8.
[60] See *The Independent*, 26th June 1996.
[61] Erskine May, *The Law, Privileges, Proceedings and Usage of Parliament* (21st edn, 1989), p 479.

meet its self-imposed legislative timetable. Many members of the House of Commons hold firmly to the traditional view of parliamentary sovereignty and would endeavour to amend or defeat any clause which sought to entrench provisions of the Act. Members of the House of Lords would do likewise. Valuable parliamentary time would be wasted – time which would be more productively spent on other provisions of the bill or on other legislation.

Mr Robertson argued that it would be far easier and far less time-consuming to have a solemn Declaration of Parliament. Such a Declaration, however, would be equivalent to a resolution of both Houses of Parliament. It would not have the status of law and would not be justiciable. The protection afforded by such a strategy would be extremely limited. True, without a suspension of standing orders, the House of Commons would not be able to rescind (a rarely used power) or amend the resolution in the same session,[62] but there is nothing to prevent the Commons from doing so in a subsequent session.[63] Minor modifications may be permitted within the same session, provided the substance of the resolution remains unaltered.[64] It will be argued by traditionalist and revisionist constitutional lawyers alike that a mere Declaration has no legal significance, but constitutional theory must, as so often, give way in the face of practical politics. A bolder step might be to insert a declaratory clause into the Scotland Bill, saying its effect would be 'for all time coming', but again the amount of parliamentary effort required to enact it would be great and the enforcement of such a provision by the courts is, as we have seen, at best uncertain.[65]

It is interesting to observe that no attempt was made to entrench the Northern Ireland Parliament in the Government of Ireland Act 1920. There have, however, been two mechanisms devised by the United Kingdom Parliament to 'entrench' the constitutional position of Northern Ireland as part of the United Kingdom. Section 1(2) of the Ireland Act 1949 provided:

> 'It is hereby declared that Northern Ireland remains part of His Majesty's dominions and of the United Kingdom and it is hereby affirmed that in no event will Northern Ireland or any part thereof cease to be part of His Majesty's dominions and of the United Kingdom without the consent of the Parliament of Northern Ireland.'

This was in the context of the Irish Republic ceasing to be part of His Majesty's dominions. The Stormont Parliament had a Unionist majority

---

[62] Erskine May, note 60 above, p 363.
[63] The Clerk of the House of Commons, Mr Donald Limon, maintains that 'any resolution is amendable by a subsequent motion in a later session' (authors' correspondence with the Clerk).
[64] Erskine May, note 60 above, at p 363.
[65] The Union of Great Britain and Ireland Act 1800 also stated it would be 'in force and have effect for ever', but many of its articles have been repealed or substantially amended by the UK Parliament.

throughout its existence. There would have been no doubt as to how such a vote would have gone.

A different approach was adopted in the mid-1970s. A referendum under the Northern Ireland (Border Poll) Act 1972 was held in 1973, asking the question: 'Do you want Northern Ireland to remain part of the United Kingdom?' With an almost universal Nationalist boycott, it was not surprising that the result was a resounding 'Yes'. After the prorogation of Stormont, a new declaratory provision on Northern Ireland's status within the United Kingdom was enacted, fully embracing the referendum strategy. Section 1 of the Northern Ireland Constitution Act 1973 states:

'It is hereby declared that Northern Ireland remains part of Her Majesty's dominions and of the United Kingdom, and it is hereby affirmed that in no event will Northern Ireland or any part of it cease to be part of Her Majesty's dominions and of the United Kingdom without the consent of the majority of the people of Northern Ireland voting in a poll held for the purposes of this section in accordance with Schedule 1 to this Act.'

Paragraph 1 of Sched 1 to the 1973 Act provides:

'The Secretary of State may by order direct the holding of a poll for the purposes of section 1 of this Act on a date specified in the order, but the date so specified shall not be earlier than 9th March 1983 or earlier than ten years after the date of a previous poll under this Schedule.'

The Government's intention was to measure support for Northern Ireland continuing to remain in the Union by regular referendums. Primary legislation to provide for the question and procedures to be followed would not be necessary; this would be done by subordinate legislation, with its more limited parliamentary scrutiny. Paragraph 3 of Sched 1 provides:

'The power to make orders under this Schedule includes power to vary or revoke a previous order and shall be exercisable by statutory instrument but no such order shall be made unless a draft of the order has been approved by resolution of each House of Parliament.'

Practical politics brought about the announcement by the Labour Party that a Labour Government would hold a pre-legislative referendum of the Scottish people on the principle of establishing a Scottish Parliament with tax-varying powers. It is clear that a majority vote in favour might have just as much success in protecting the Scotland Act from repeal by a subsequent Act (at least in the short term) as a section which attempted to entrench the Act. It would promote great moral and political entrenchment.[66] The West-

---

[66] See J. MacCormick and W. Alexander in S. Tindale (ed), *The State and the Nations* (IPPR, 1996), p 125: 'A positive referendum result cannot deliver constitutional entrenchment, but it might be seen as a tactical resource in strengthening moral and political entrenchment ... if the Scottish Parliament cannot convince the public it is relevant to their lives, entrenchment will neither be possible or deserved.'

minster Parliament might be more likely to believe that a Scottish Parliament which had been established after consulting the Scottish people should not be abolished without consulting the Scottish people. It has been argued that the entrenching effect of any such referendum would become progressively less over time.[67] If, however, a provision similar to s 1 of the Northern Ireland Constitution Act 1973 were adopted, involving regular referendums in the future, there would be practical difficulties in expecting the Scottish electorate to vote in potentially limitless referendums simply to preserve their new constitutional settlement – not least the possibility of voter apathy or fatigue.

Could either of the two Northern Ireland approaches be adapted to Scotland's requirements? Aside from the inherent differences between these two parts of the United Kingdom, adopting the approach of the Ireland Act 1949 is clearly unsuitable. After establishing a Scottish Parliament following a referendum in Scotland, it is unreasonable to give the Scottish Parliament the ability to declare independence from the United Kingdom or to seek its own abolition by a mere parliamentary vote, without consulting the Scottish people in a referendum to see whether such a proposition would have their consent. Elections to the Scottish Parliament could produce a majority of pro-independence or anti-devolution members, who might have been elected primarily on other issues, such as health, education or unemployment in Scotland. Very rarely are parliamentary elections simply referendums on constitutional issues. Declaring a mandate for separation or for abolition of the Scottish Parliament on the basis of the outcome of an election to the Scottish Parliament would be unfair and unreasonable.

A modification of the approach of the Northern Ireland Constitution Act 1973 seems to be more suitable. A possible solution is to make any *substantial* proposed changes to the constitutional position of Scotland within the United Kingdom subject to a future referendum, occurring only where a government proposed outright abolition of the Scottish Parliament, or independence from the United Kingdom. Does this require legislative expression or not? A simple statement of policy from the Government adopting the above position might well suffice. Disregarding the question of whether or not there should be a generic Referendum Act for the United Kingdom,[68] a key consideration is which Parliament should have the power to activate and hold such a referendum. The Westminster Parliament may be of the opinion that, as it would

---

[67] See, eg, Scotland's Parliament: Fundamentals for a Scotland Act (Constitution Unit, 1996), p 51 *et seq.*

[68] A possibility discussed in the report of the Commission for Electoral Reform and the Constitution Unit, Report of the Commission on the Conduct of Referendums (1996).

have overall responsibility for the constitution of the United Kingdom, it should have the power to hold such a referendum and determine the question or questions to be put, but there are precedents indicating that it might be more suitable for the Scottish Parliament to exercise this referendum power.

Local authorities have a power to 'conduct, or assist in the conducting of, investigations into, and the collection of information relating to, any matters concerning their area or any part thereof and may make, or assist in the making of, arrangements whereby any such information and the results of any such investigation are made available to any government department or the public'.[69] This power was used by Strathclyde Regional Council to hold a referendum in early 1994 as to whether the public considered that water should be taken out of local authority control in Scotland. The Scotland Act 1978 did not confer such a power on the putative Scottish Assembly, although ministers in the Scottish Assembly could be compelled to provide the Secretary of State for Scotland with information pertaining to the exercise of their functions.[70] There is no reason, however, why a future Scotland Bill should not contain a provision permitting the Scottish Parliament to conduct investigations into any sphere of its operation, which could incorporate the use of a referendum on the constitution. This could be a general enabling provision, leaving the form of the question(s) and the procedures to be utilised to be determined by an Act of the Scottish Parliament.

That is one option. The United Kingdom Parliament might not wish to give the Scottish Parliament so broad a power. The legislation could therefore provide that the power be made subject to consultation with, or the approval of, say, a liaison committee of the Scottish and United Kingdom Parliaments. Another possibility is to leave the power to call a referendum on the constitution with Westminster, and have it triggered by a recommendation of this inter-parliamentary committee. Whichever of the options is eventually approved, there is clearly an advantage in deciding the issue when the Scotland Bill is before Parliament, rather than leaving it to possibly acrimonious dispute between the Parliaments at a later stage. The decision whether to include such a clause in the Scotland Bill is a difficult one, in which clarity and a possible bulwark for the Union falls to be balanced against the time spent debating such a clause in Parliament.

The most important long-term practical safeguard would undoubtedly be a change in the voting system of the United Kingdom Parliament away from the current 'first past the post' to a more proportionate system, making the repeal

---

[69] Section 87(1) of the Local Government (Scotland) Act 1973, as amended by para 21(a) of Sched 13 to the Local Government etc (Scotland) Act 1994.

[70] Section 36.

or amendment of such constitutional legislation more difficult, because of the
greater likelihood of coalition governments, which would make it more difficult
for extreme views to achieve legislative expression.

A Bill of Rights and entrenchment

Even more difficult questions of sovereignty and entrenchment would arise if
the United Kingdom Parliament were to enact a Bill of Rights. Could such an
enactment be entrenched and would the United Kingdom courts be able to
police it effectively? The issue was considered in 1977–78 by the House of
Lords Select Committee on a Bill of Rights which addressed the arguments on
entrenchment examined above. The Committee concluded that

> 'there is no way in which a Bill of Rights could protect itself from encroachment,
> whether express or implied by later Acts. The most that such a bill could do would be
> to include an interpretation provision which ensured that a Bill of Rights was always
> taken into account in the construction of later Acts, and that so far as a later Act could
> be construed in a way that was compatible with a Bill of Rights, such a construction
> would be preferred to one that was not'.[71]

Another suggestion is that a Bill of Rights might contain a 'notwithstanding'
clause – that is, a form of words attempting to bar implied repeal – another
possible technique to protect the provisions of the Scotland Act. The House of
Lords Select Committee, however, considered that this solution was excluded
by the decisions in *Vauxhall Estates* and *Ellen Street Estates*.[72]

About a decade ago, the New Zealand Government began the process of
drawing up and enacting a Bill of Rights.[73] In Parliament, the same doubts were
raised as to whether, in a system without a written constitution, a Bill of Rights
could be enacted that would be protected from amendment by an ordinary Act
of Parliament. The only precedent for an entrenched provision that existed in
New Zealand statute law was itself unprotected from future repeal by a hostile
Parliament acting by simple majority.[74] Relying on the three Commonwealth
'manner-and-form' decisions considered above, a change of mind by New
Zealand constitutional lawyers, and the 'practical sanctity' of political consensus,
entrenchment was at least floated as a viable option in the consultation process
sparked by the White Paper, A Bill of Rights for New Zealand.[75] Article 28 of the
draft Bill of Rights stated that no provision of the bill could be amended or in any

---

[71] (1977–78) HL 176 at para 23; and see memorandum of D. Rippengal on entrenchment
  (1977–78) HL 81, pp 1–10.
[72] See footnotes 5 and 6 above.
[73] Finally enacting the New Zealand Bill of Rights Act 1990.
[74] Section 189 of the Electoral Act 1956, which provided that the law relating to voting age and
  method of voting could only be altered by a proposal receiving the support of 75% of the total
  membership of the House of Representatives, or approval in a referendum.
[75] At p 57.

way affected unless the proposal to do so were passed by a three-quarters majority of the House of Representatives, or had been approved in a referendum by the people. When the Draft Bill went before the Justice and Law Reform Select Committee, it was argued by the Committee that 'in our view entrenchment is necessary to ensure that the Bill is durable'.[76]

But arguments for a provision to enable the New Zealand Parliament to have a right of override were also advanced, and by the time of the final report, art 28 had disappeared, and with it the attempt to entrench the Bill of Rights. The concept of parliamentary override had been embraced.[77] More recently, the Master of the Rolls, Lord Woolf of Barnes, has expressed his personal view that a non-entrenched Bill of Rights on the New Zealand model, and with a right of parliamentary override, could fit comfortably with the British tradition of parliamentary sovereignty.[78]

If a future United Kingdom Parliament attempts to enact a Bill of Rights, this is more likely to resolve such dilemmas of parliamentary sovereignty than the enactment of a Scotland Act. A proposal to enact a Bill of Rights, and the debate over whether it should be entrenched or not, would bring to the fore fundamental questions about the power of the courts to review, and possibly strike down, legislation enacted by Parliament. A Bill of Rights might provoke a debate about whether Parliament should be limited and subject to some form of higher law in the domestic sphere and about whether sovereignty rests in Parliament or in the people of Britain. To make the people rather than Parliament sovereign in the strict legal sense, and not in the sense of self-determination for the regions and nations of the United Kingdom, only a written constitution adopted by a Constituent Assembly of both Houses of Parliament following the appropriate legislation and a referendum will suffice.[79] The practical difficulties in reaching that position should be obvious. It is not on the current political agenda.

Conclusions

In practical terms parliamentary sovereignty has become crystallised in the constitution of the United Kingdom, consisting of rules that have become fundamental to our system of government. The reality is that the doctrine of the sovereignty of Parliament will continue well into the next millennium, long after any Scottish Parliament will have been established, with all the

[76] Inquiry into the White Paper – A Bill of Rights for New Zealand (1986), p 73.
[77] Final Report of the Justice and Law Reform Committee on a White Paper on a Bill of Rights for New Zealand (1988), p 3.
[78] 'Droit Public – English Style' [1995] PL 57 at p 70.
[79] Along the lines of Hood Phillips's proposals in *Reform of the Constitution* (1970).

implications that that has for entrenchment of the legislation. The 'popular sovereignty' of a bygone age cannot be revived. A pre-legislative referendum in Scotland on our constitutional future could well be the most suitable modern-day embodiment of popular sovereignty. The firmest entrenchment could come from a new voting system, bringing about a dramatic change in our political culture, and creating a new practical brake on sovereignty. In the short to medium term though, a clause similar to s 1 of the Northern Ireland Constitution Act 1973 is perfectly workable, and could go a long way towards meeting objections that a Scottish Parliament within the United Kingdom could lead to a process of separation; the parliamentary considerations of having a relatively slim Scotland Bill going through Parliament as quickly as possible could well prove equally attractive to an incoming government with a heavy legislative workload. That is the balance to be struck by Parliament. The fundamental truth about devolution for Scotland is that entrenchment in the hearts and minds of the Scottish people will be the most crucial factor in determining the powers and longevity of a Scottish Parliament – a distinctly political issue, just as it always has been.

Parliaments and Courts: Powers and Dispute Resolution

Colin Boyd, QC

Introduction

The establishment of a Scottish Parliament could bring about the most profound constitutional change in Britain since the Irish Free State left the Union in 1922. As envisaged by the Scottish Constitutional Convention, the Parliament will be a powerful domestic legislature with wide powers over a broad range of devolved matters. If approved in the pre-legislative referendum, the Parliament will have the power to vary the standard rate of income tax by up to three pence in the pound. Yet Scotland will remain part of the United Kingdom. The Westminster Parliament will retain powers over such things as foreign affairs and defence, macro-economic and fiscal policy, social security and immigration. How will the two legislatures relate to each other? And how will disputes between them and their respective governments be resolved?

The Scottish Parliament will be a creation of statute. It will be for the British Parliament to enact legislation which establishes the Parliament for Scotland. Its powers and competence will be derived from that legislation. The Act of Parliament will prescribe what the Scottish Parliament can do and proscribe those areas which are beyond its competence. The Act will also set out what the Scottish Government can and cannot do. Accordingly, each measure passed by the Scottish Parliament and every action of a Scottish minister may be tested against the primary legislation to see whether or not it is within the competence of the Parliament or of the minister.

The Scottish Parliament will, therefore, be a subordinate parliament. Its powers will be laid down in an Act of the United Kingdom Parliament. Its actings will be the subject of administrative and judicial scrutiny. It will be very different to the United Kingdom Parliament whose actings, traditionally, cannot be scrutinised by a court. In British or, perhaps, more accurately, English, constitutional theory, Parliament is sovereign. It has the right to make or unmake laws and no person has the right to override or set aside legislation made by the United Kingdom Parliament.

It would appear, therefore, that although legislation passed by the Scottish

Parliament could be the subject of judicial scrutiny, Acts of the United Kingdom Parliament could not be questioned in a judicial process even if that Act dealt with a devolution issue. However, as Jean McFadden and William Bain have shown, the theory of parliamentary sovereignty as enunciated by Dicey[1] has been the subject of review by jurists and by the courts. British membership of the European Communities has meant that the courts have had to accept that by enacting the European Communities Act 1972, Parliament bound itself not to pass legislation which conflicted with obligations incurred under the European treaties, at least without repealing or amending that Act.[2] The United Kingdom Parliament could, in a similar manner, attempt to bind itself not to pass legislation which conflicted with the terms of the devolution Act which established the Scottish Parliament.

There are three ways in which the British Parliament could seek to limit its future freedom of action as a consequence of establishing a Scottish Parliament. The first would be to provide in the devolution Act that the Scottish Parliament could not be abolished without some form of consent being established for abolition. That consent could come from the Scottish Parliament itself, or from the Scottish electorate expressed through a referendum held for that purpose. Of course abolition of the Scottish Parliament, should that be contemplated, would be done by repealing the devolution Act. Since the repeal of the devolution Act would also repeal the provision for consent it would in theory be open to the Westminster Parliament simply to ignore the need to obtain consent. To some this means that such a provision is not worth incorporating in the Act. On the other hand, it would at least put into legislative form a political commitment to guarantee the long-term future of the Scottish Parliament. It would send a political message in much the same way as the provision in the Northern Ireland Constitution Act 1973 which declares that Northern Ireland remains part of the United Kingdom and that in no event shall it cease to be part of the United Kingdom without the consent of a majority of the people of Northern Ireland.

Secondly, the Act could provide that there would be no derogation from the powers of the Scottish Parliament without consent. For example, if the parliament is given tax-raising powers these could not be taken away without the consent of the Scottish Parliament or the Scottish people in a referendum.

Another possibility is that Parliament may provide that it may not legislate in areas reserved to the Scottish Parliament without its consent. It may be assumed that the United Kingdom Parliament would not ordinarily wish to

---

[1] A. V. Dicey, *Introduction to the Study of the Law of the Constitution*, ch 1.

[2] See *R v Secretary of State for Transport, ex parte Factortame Ltd* [1990] 2 AC 85.

enact legislation in devolved areas unless absolutely necessary. But so long as it adheres to the principle of parliamentary sovereignty without qualification it would, in theory, retain the right to do so. The incorporation of a provision which required the consent of the Scottish Parliament before the United Kingdom Parliament could legislate in a devolved area would mean that if the consent was not forthcoming, or was not sought, the United Kingdom Parliament would have to repeal or amend the provision which required that consent in the devolution Act. It may well be reluctant to take that step. Apart from the political message which that might have it would also mean that Westminster could not legislate in a devolved area 'by accident'. It would either require consent from the Scottish Parliament or it would have to amend the devolution Act specifically. The one occasion on which such consent would not be required would be where the legislation was necessary in order to comply with an international obligation of the United Kingdom.

Whether the United Kingdom Parliament would be willing to fetter its powers in these ways must be open to doubt. The Scottish Constitutional Convention accepted in its report that it was not open to the United Kingdom Parliament to entrench the Scottish Parliament. It appears to have been advised on this by the Scottish Constitutional Commission. That advice may be open to question but, in any event, the Convention opted instead for a solemn declaration to be made by Parliament that the Act founding the Scottish Parliament should not be amended or repealed without the consent of the Scottish Parliament or the Scottish people.[3] Such a declaration would have no legal status or binding effect.

The distinction between a declaration of Parliament and a provision requiring consent before certain actions were taken is important. A declaration of Parliament would not confer any justiciable rights, whereas a provision which required consent before, for example, the United Kingdom Parliament could legislate in a devolved area could confer rights which were capable of judicial recognition. If the United Kingdom Parliament attempted to amend the powers of the Scottish Parliament or to legislate in a devolved area without the consent of the Scottish Parliament (or, if appropriate, the Scottish people in a referendum), that may give rise to a challenge which could be made in a court of law. The procedures which the devolution Act sets out for reviewing the legislation of the Scottish Parliament and the resolution of the disputes between the Scottish and British Parliaments would necessarily have to include the possibility that challenges may be made to Acts of the United Kingdom Parliament. That would not be necessary if Parliament were to adopt a

---

[3] Scotland's Parliament: Scotland's Right (Scottish Constitutional Convention, 1995).

declaration instead, though challenges may be brought to acts of United Kingdom ministers under the devolution Act.

General principles

In attempting to delineate areas of responsibility and establish procedures for review and resolution of disputes it is suggested that a number of general principles should be followed.

First, the Scottish Parliament and Government should be allowed, within the scope of the legislation, to get on with the job without interference from outside. There will be times, particularly arising from United Kingdom obligations to the European Union, when the British Government will wish to take an interest in areas which are devolved to the Scottish Parliament. However, conflict could arise if the British institutions are seen to be interfering in what are thought by the Scottish Parliament and Government to be exclusively within their competence. Much will depend not only on the political complexion of the two legislatures but the personalities involved. However, it is suggested that the right to intervene or challenge the decisions of the Scottish institutions should be confined to those occasions on which it is alleged that they are acting outwith their powers or that they are compromising an international obligation of the United Kingdom.

Secondly, the Act which establishes the Scottish Parliament should be as clear and precise as possible in defining devolved matters and setting out the rights and obligations of the institutions involved. This is not the place to consider the powers that parliament may have. There are, however, two basic methods of defining these powers. The first is to list the areas of legislative and executive competence which are devolved to the Scottish institutions. This was the method adopted by the Scotland Act 1978 where Scheds 10 and 11 listed the powers which were transferred to the Scottish Assembly and Executive. It has been argued that this approach, although a tempting starting-point, was too detailed for its own good.[4] The Schedules were difficult to understand and open to different interpretations. The Scottish Assembly would have had to point to the specific head of power in which it proposed to legislate. The alternative method, which the Government of Ireland Act 1920 adopted, is to list the reserved powers and allow the Scottish Parliament to legislate in any area not reserved. This approach would be clearer and easier for ordinary people, let alone lawyers, to understand. It is less likely to lead to disputes and litigation. The Scottish Parliament would not have to point to a particular

[4] Scotland's Parliament: Laying the Foundations (The Constitution Unit's Report on Scottish Devolution).

provision to justify the legislation. Psychologically it would help establish it as a responsible body.

Thirdly, where disputes arise and cannot be resolved by negotiation they should be resolved by a judicial body and not by politicians. This is particularly important where questions arise in the course of litigation or the rights of individual citizens are involved. Any form of judicial or quasi-judicial arbitration which relies on politicians or seeks to involve them in the resolution process risks the charge that the process is tainted by attempts to gain political advantage or that objectivity has been clouded by proximity to the dispute. Accordingly the determination must be made by a court of law.

Fourthly, the judicial body exercising the responsibility for resolving the dispute should be one in which the parties to the dispute have confidence, whether they be the legislatures, governments or private individuals. It is important also that the wider public in Scotland as well as the rest of the United Kingdom accept the body as being fair and judicial. This will involve choosing the right body and also ensuring that the composition of the court is seen to be fair and not 'packed'. It may be that this latter point is one which is taken care of by convention; ensuring that there are Scottish judges well represented within the members of the court determining the issue.

Finally, a system for resolving disputes should, so far as possible, be quick and efficient. A system which drags out the dispute is of no advantage to anyone.

Pre-assent scrutiny and review

Under the Scotland Act 1978 the Assembly could make laws which were entitled Scottish Assembly Acts. Proposed Scottish Assembly Acts were known as bills and a bill become an Act when it had been passed by the Assembly and approved by Her Majesty in Council.[5] It appears to have been the duty of the Secretary of State to submit the bill passed by the Assembly to Her Majesty in Council for approval.[6]

It is likely that the procedure for enacting legislation will follow the same method as in the Scotland Act 1978, though it would not be necessary for the submission for the Royal Assent to be made by the Secretary of State. It could be done by the Scottish Prime Minister or the Presiding Officer of the Scottish Parliament.

The Act also provided for the scrutiny of every bill passed by the Assembly by the Secretary of State.[7] If he was of the opinion that any of the bill's

[5] Section 17.
[6] Section 19(4).
[7] Section 19(1).

provisions were not within the legislative competence of the Assembly he was to refer that question to the Judicial Committee of the Privy Council for its decision. He could also refer the question where he was of the opinion that there was sufficient doubt about it to justify a reference. If the Judicial Committee decided that any provision of a bill was not within the legislative competence of the Assembly, the Secretary of State could not submit the bill for Royal Assent. If, on the other hand, the Judicial Committee decided that a provision was within the legislative competence of the Assembly, the decision was binding in all legal proceedings.[8]

A pre-assent right to review proposed legislation appears to be a sensible approach. Situations may occur where there is a clear and readily ascertainable dispute as to whether the particular provisions of a bill are within the legislative competence of the Scottish Parliament. It seems right that that dispute should not be allowed to continue with the enacting of legislation about which there is a real question as to the competence of the Scottish Parliament to enact it. That will only make for uncertainty.

On the other hand, it seems unnecessary to provide that the Secretary of State must consider every bill passed by the Scottish Parliament. It is demeaning to the parliament to have enacted in the devolution Act a provision that every piece of legislation will be monitored. It strongly suggests that the Scottish Parliament cannot be trusted to act responsibly. In practice each bill will no doubt be considered by the British Government. It needs no statutory authority to do so. If a question about the *vires* of a particular bill is going to be raised it is likely that it will have been the subject of political debate beforehand and the bill can be referred to the appropriate political body after being passed by the parliament but before receiving the Royal Assent.

Membership of the European Union brings other problems, which are addressed here and also in St John Bates's paper. Although procedures may well be put in place to allow for the representation of the views of the Scottish Parliament and Government to the institutions of the European Union, the responsibility for fulfilling the obligations imposed by the European treaties on the United Kingdom remain the responsibility of the United Kingdom Government. A method has to be found for ensuring that the Scottish Parliament does nothing that would be incompatible with the United Kingdom's international and in particular European obligations.

Under s 19(2) of the 1978 Act, if the Secretary of State was of the opinion that the bill was not in conformity with Community or other international obligations of the United Kingdom, or that it provided for matters which were

---

[8] Section 19(4).

or ought to be provided for by or under legislation passed by Parliament and implementing such obligations, he was required to certify to the Assembly that he was of that opinion and not submit it to Her Majesty for approval. Thus the bill was measured not only against existing British legislation implementing Community and other international obligations but was also against the desirability of Westminster legislating on these matters whether or not such legislation was contemplated at the time of certification. There was no mechanism for review of the Secretary of State's decision.

With the growing volume of European legislation the scope for use of this power in the present day may not be insignificant. If a British Secretary of State took the view that it was more desirable to implement a European directive by legislating in the Westminster Parliament rather than in the Scottish Parliament he could certify that fact and prevent a Scottish bill from being enacted.

Community obligations are defined in the European Communities Act 1972[9] as 'any obligation created or arising under the Treaties, whether an enforceable Community obligation or not'. Thus a Community obligation covers obligations which have direct effect and are enforceable in United Kingdom law under s 2(1) of the 1972 Act (that is, without further legislation by Parliament), and obligations which do not have direct effect in United Kingdom law but are owed to the European Union by the United Kingdom as a member of the European Union.[10]

In the debate in the House of Lords on this provision in the 1978 Act[11] it was suggested that where it appeared that a provision in an Assembly bill was incompatible with an obligation having direct effect, that should be referred to the Judicial Committee. Lord McCluskey, then the Solicitor-General for Scotland, argued against such a proposal, suggesting that it would force the government to declare whether or not, in its opinion, an obligation was one having direct effect. It was also suggested that there would be the further possible step of a reference to the European Court of Justice under art 177 of the Treaty. This, he argued, would delay matters further. Despite the government's opposition, the House of Lords passed an amendment which would have had the effect of referring such questions to the Judicial Committee. However, the House of Commons did not accept the amendment and it was not part of the Scotland Act.

Given the range and scope of legislation from the European Union, which has grown both in volume and importance since Lord McCluskey addressed

---

[9] Section 1(2) and Sched 1.
[10] European Communities Act 1972, s 2.
[11] Hansard HL, vol 390, cols 119–141 (18th April 1978).

the issue, it seems unsatisfactory that this should not be referred to a judicial body for determination. If it is simply up to a British minister to decide that there is a conflict, there remains a potential for abuse since few areas of government remain unaffected by the obligations imposed by the European Union.

Accordingly, there are strong reasons for suggesting that where a bill is alleged to be incompatible with a Community obligation having direct effect, or which may have direct effect, it should be referred to a judicial body for a decision. If it is incompatible with such an obligation, then, to the extent that it is incompatible, it should be outwith the competence of the Scottish Parliament and accordingly null and void.

Questions might still arise about obligations which did not have direct effect. Mechanisms will require to be put in place which deal with obligations of the United Kingdom to the European Union and other international bodies. These may require either a positive action by the Scottish Parliament in enacting legislation which is within its competence or a negative action in not enacting legislation in conflict with such obligations. In part these could be dealt with by reserving to the United Kingdom Parliament the right to legislate in devolved areas where it is necessary to do so in order to meet an international obligation.

However, it may also be necessary to provide the United Kingdom Parliament with an override power to veto a bill which the Scottish Parliament insists on passing and which conflicts with Britain's international obligations. It is suggested, however, that such a right of veto should be strictly defined and, in order to prevent any possible abuse, it should be subject to review by a judicial body.

This would contrast with the position under the Scotland Act 1978 which gave Westminster a wide power to reject certain bills with no mechanism for judicial review. If it appeared to the Secretary of State that a bill passed by the Assembly contained any provision which 'would or might affect a reserved matter whether directly or indirectly; and ... that the enactment of that provision would not be in the public interest',[12] he could lay the bill before Parliament, together with a reasoned statement that, in his opinion, it ought not to be submitted to Her Majesty for approval. A reserved matter was one which affected Scotland (whether or not it concerned any other part of the United Kingdom) and was a matter in respect of which the Scottish Assembly had no power to legislate.[13] If both Houses of Parliament resolved that the bill

---

[12] Section 38(1); emphasis added.
[13] Section 38(2).

should not be submitted to Her Majesty in Council for approval, it was not to be so submitted.[14]

The power appears to be wide. There may have been few matters upon which the Scottish Assembly could legislate in which it could not have been said that it would not affect, or might not affect, directly or indirectly, a reserved matter. It is true that the Secretary of State had a discretion as to whether or not to lay the bill before Parliament, seeking authority not to submit it for Royal Assent, and that before he did so he had to be satisfied that the enactment of the provision would not be in the public interest. Nevertheless, there seems to be no reason to suppose that a British Secretary of State is a better guardian of the public interest than the Scottish Parliament. And the question as to whether a Scottish bill might or might not affect a reserved matter and therefore be outwith the competence of the Scottish Parliament is one that can and should be determined by a court of law.

There may be a case for providing that someone other than a Secretary of State should be responsible for making a reference to a judicial body. First, it may be that the office of Secretary of State for Scotland will not be required after devolution, certainly in the long term. In his absence it is not clear which Secretary of State might exercise that function. Secondly, there is a case for providing that the function of referring a bill to a judicial body for scrutiny should be undertaken by a law officer. Although a Secretary of State would no doubt act on the advice of a law officer, there may nevertheless be a temptation for referrals to be made for political reasons rather than strictly constitutional purposes. A law officer may be perceived as bringing an independent professional assessment to a constitutional question. The fact that a reference has been made by someone exercising a legal judgment may be more acceptable to the Scottish Parliament and to Scottish public opinion. If the Lord Advocate remains a minister of the United Kingdom Government, the function could be undertaken by him. If the Lord Advocate becomes a minister of the Scottish Government, the United Kingdom minister exercising the function of law officer for Scotland could initiate the referral.

Accordingly, there should be a simple, fast and effective method of testing the *vires* of a bill of the Scottish Parliament prior to it being submitted to Her Majesty in Council for approval. That would determine whether or not the bill was within the legislative competence of the Scottish Parliament and would include questions as to whether the bill conflicted with European obligations having direct effect. The provision would enable a reference to be made to a judicial body where, in the opinion of the person making the reference, the bill

[14] Section 38(3).

was not within the legislative competence of the Scottish Parliament or conflicted with a European obligation having direct effect, or that there was sufficient doubt about the matter to justify a reference. That provision would be similar to s 19(1) of the 1978 Act.

There could also be provision for a right of veto to be exercised by the Westminster Parliament where it could be shown that the Bill conflicted with an international obligation of the United Kingdom. Such a right would be strictly defined and itself open to review by a judicial body.

If the devolution Act provides that certain Acts of the United Kingdom Parliament required the consent of the Scottish Parliament, or the Scottish electorate in a referendum, the possibility arises for scrutinising bills passed by the United Kingdom Parliament prior to their receiving the Royal Assent. Scrutiny before enactment would not be necessary; as with legislation which might conflict with European legislation it could be left in place until a court decided that the Act, or part of it, was outwith the powers of the United Kingdom Parliament, unless it first repealed or amended the provision for consent in the devolution Act. However, questions could arise as to whether the United Kingdom Parliament was legislating in a devolved area and, if it was, whether the bill had received the requisite consent, or whether the proposed legislation was necessary to fulfil an international obligation. These questions could be determined prior to the bill being submitted for the Royal Assent. In that event it would be necessary to provide a means of referring the United Kingdom bill to the court of review. That reference could be made by the Scottish Parliament itself, a Scottish minister, or a law officer.

It is unlikely that a pre-assent scrutiny of Scottish Parliament bills by a court of review would be used often. In many cases the issue will have been the subject of political debate before passing through the parliamentary stages. Often the potential conflict may well have been resolved through negotiation. The comparable procedure under s 51 of the Government of Ireland Act was used only once.[15]

The court of review

The question then arises as to which judicial body should referrals be made. There may be merit, as Gordon Jackson has argued, in the establishment of a constitutional court or council to determine these issues. In many European countries constitutional questions are determined by a special constitutional body established for that purpose. In other countries, such as the United

---

[15] *Re a Reference under the Government of Ireland Act 1920* [1936] AC 352.

States, a supreme or high court exercises these functions alongside the function of ultimate court of appeal.

In the House of Lords debate on the Scotland Bill,[16] Lord Wilberforce moved an amendment to the effect that devolution issues should be referred to a constitutional court. His suggestion was that it should consist of seven members and that as well as professional judges such as Lords of Appeal there should be experts in constitutional law such as professors. They would, apparently, have been appointed for three years. The amendment was supported by Lord Wilson of Langside, a former Lord Advocate. Lord Diplock opposed it, saying that it struck at the root of the Act of Settlement. It is clear from his speech that Lord Wilberforce saw this as another step in reforming the constitution and perhaps heralding further development. Of course, other constitutional reforms are being considered. The European Convention on Human Rights may be incorporated into United Kingdom law, giving us, however imperfectly, a Bill of Rights. The House of Lords may be reformed or replaced. Devolution to the English regions is being considered. All of these reforms may give rise to calls for a constitutional court and one can see that, as such developments take place, so might the pressure to consider reform of the way in which constitutional issues are determined.

However, such a proposal is unlikely to commend itself to Parliament at the present time. There is no widespread clamour for it either publicly or in legal circles. It is not suggested that there is not a court which could deal with constitutional issues and it seems unnecessary to invent one to deal only with devolution issues. These in themselves would not warrant the appointment of a full-time court. Moreover, the constitution of the court might itself give rise to considerable debate, diverting attention from the real issue of establishing a Scottish Parliament.

In the absence of a constitutional court there are two possibilities: one is the House of Lords and the other the Judicial Committee of the Privy Council. It may be said that there is little difference between them since the judges are usually the same. In the same House of Lords debate Lord Hailsham said that the difference between the two was a large Daimler car which was used to convey their Lordships between the House of Lords and the Privy Council offices in Downing Street. Both bodies have merits and drawbacks. On the one hand the House of Lords is the ultimate court of appeal in Scotland for civil matters (but not criminal matters). It is perhaps the closest to a supreme court. Two of the Lords of Appeal in Ordinary are Scottish lawyers and they may be supplemented by other members of the House of Lords who hold or have held

[16] Hansard HL, vol 390, cols 1087–1118 (18th April 1978).

high judicial office. Thus the former Lord President of the Court of Session sat in the House of Lords Appellate Committee before his appointment as a Lord of Appeal.

On the other hand, there was, historically, great resistance to the idea that the House of Lords should have any function in Scottish appeals. Acceptance of the fact has, perhaps, been grudging rather than welcomed. It would give the House of Lords a role in Scottish criminal matters which it has not had before. There is also the perception that the House of Lords is part of the Parliament of the United Kingdom and would therefore be, on occasion, judge in its own cause. Lawyers will appreciate the distinction between the Appellate Committee and the House of Lords as a whole, but the general public may not be so easily convinced.

The Privy Council, it is suggested, is the natural place for devolution questions to be decided. It was where devolution issues were to be decided under the Scotland Act 1978. Section 51 of the Government of Ireland Act 1920 provided for referrals to the Judicial Committee of the Privy Council to consider whether any Act of the Parliaments of Northern or Southern Ireland was beyond the powers of that parliament. The Northern Ireland Constitution Act 1973 provided that any measure of the Northern Ireland Assembly or Act of the Parliament of Northern Ireland would, to the extent that it discriminated against any person or class of persons on the grounds of religious belief or political opinion, be void.[17] The Secretary of State could refer such a question to the Judicial Committee of the Privy Council for a decision.[18] The Privy Council has been the ultimate court of appeal from dominions and colonies and in the process has dealt with constitutional issues – for example, between Canadian provinces and the Federal government. It has a wider membership, including some Commonwealth judges. Its membership could be easily augmented by creating Privy Councillors without having to create Life Peers.

Post-assent challenges

The Scotland Act 1978 provided for challenges to the *vires* of Acts of the Scottish Assembly even after they had received the Royal Assent. Some debate has taken place as to whether it is appropriate to allow post-assent challenges. It has been suggested that to do so would introduce an element of uncertainty into the law producing undesirable consequences. An Act of the Scottish Parliament would remain an Act only so long as it was unchallenged.

[17] Section 17.
[18] Section 18.

However, this argument does not stand up to detailed scrutiny. Challenges to subordinate legislation are not uncommon and the matters dealt with by statutory instrument can be of great significance. Moreover, we now have challenges to legislation based on the contention that it does not conform to obligations under the treaties establishing the European Union. It would be an anomaly to allow for an Act of Parliament to be found not to be in conformity with European obligations and thus inoperative but not to allow for Acts of the Scottish Parliament to be found to be *ultra vires* after receiving the Royal Assent. Further, it is sometimes difficult to determine an issue in the abstract. It may be only when particular circumstances arise and the facts known that the issue of legislative competence can be addressed. Legislation may affect only a small number of people who may not have the resources to examine the legislation in detail to see whether it may affect them and, if it does, whether it is within the Scottish Parliament's competence. If post-assent challenges were not to be allowed real injustice may result. In practice the largest number of challenges are likely to be after the Royal Assent and raised in the course of other proceedings.

Schedule 12 to the 1978 Act made provision for legal proceedings involving devolution issues. The basic scheme, with some alterations, appears sensible. In the 1978 Act a devolution issue was defined as

'(a) whether a Scottish Assembly Act or any provision of a Scottish Assembly Act is within the legislative competence of the Assembly; or (b) whether a matter with respect to which a Scottish Secretary has purported to exercise or proposes to exercise a power is a devolved matter'.

That definition may be rather narrow. It excludes from consideration all actings of the United Kingdom Parliament and all actings by British ministers. A broader definition should include all questions arising from the exercise of powers or failure to exercise powers conferred by the devolution Act, whether by the Scottish or United Kingdom Parliaments or by Scottish or British ministers.

Legal proceedings for the determination of a devolution issue could be instituted and defended by the respective law officers. They may also be instituted by any person who could show a title and interest.

Devolution issues could also arise in the course of other proceedings. In civil matters, where a devolution issue is raised in legal proceedings before a court, not being the House of Lords or a court of the Court of Session consisting of three or more judges, or a tribunal, it should be referred to the Inner House of the Court of Session.

Where the Inner House makes a determination on a reference under this provision, or where it arises before the Inner House of the Court of Session, an appeal against the determination should lie to the Judicial Committee of the Privy Council. In the 1978 Act if a devolution issue arose in proceedings before the House of Lords, it was to be referred to the Judicial Committee of the Privy Council, 'unless the House considers it more appropriate, having regard to all the circumstances, that they should determine the issue'.[19] That seems a sensible approach.

Where a devolution issue is raised in criminal proceedings, it should be referred to the High Court of Justiciary consisting of at least three judges. There should be a right of appeal to the Privy Council.

Actions by ministers of the Scottish Government

Section 39 of the Scotland Act 1978 enabled the Secretary of State to direct that certain action be taken, or not taken, as the case may be, by a Scottish Secretary. The events upon which such directions could be made were when such action, or lack of action, would or might affect 'whether directly or indirectly' a reserved matter. Under subsection (2) the direction could be given where the action taken by the Scottish Secretary was incompatible with Community obligations or other international obligations of the United Kingdom. The direction could also be made where it was required to implement such an obligation. Section 64 of the Act provided that where an international obligation required the exercise of a power to make a subordinate instrument and that power could be exercised by a Scottish Secretary but it was desirable that it should be exercised by a Minister of the Crown, the Minister may exercise that power as if it were not a devolved matter.

Under s 40 the Secretary of State was given the power to revoke subordinate legislation where it affected or might affect a reserved matter directly or indirectly and was in the public interest to do so. He could also revoke such legislation where it was incompatible with a Community or other international obligation. A revocation order would cease to have effect unless within twenty-eight days of the order being made a resolution approving the order had been passed by both Houses of Parliament.

Such powers perhaps go too far. As with legislation, a provision that a Scottish minister must not take any action or make any subordinate legislation which is incompatible with European or other international obligations would be sufficient. If he purported to take such action or make such subordinate legislation, the Secretary of State or other appropriate United Kingdom minister could initiate legal proceedings to prevent such action being taken or to annul such subordinate legislation.

---

[19] Sched 12, para 24.

In the event that an action or the making of a subordinate instrument was required to enable the United Kingdom to comply with European or other international treaty obligations, the Secretary of State or other United Kingdom minister could require that action to be taken or the subordinate legislation made, failing which the action or the making of the instrument could be taken by the United Kingdom minister responsible.

Conclusions

The establishment of a Scottish Parliament provides a unique opportunity to legislate for Scotland in Scotland, to bring government closer to the people of Scotland and to provide a focus for a Scottish identity in the United Kingdom. If it is to work it is important that the powers of the Scottish Parliament and its government are well defined and that the mechanisms for the resolution of disputes is one in which all the people of the United Kingdom have confidence. The challenge for the constitutional lawyer is to provide the mechanisms. The challenge for the parliamentarians who will require to legislate is to have confidence in the ability of the British constitution to reform and provide a system of government for Scotland and the rest of the United Kingdom which can take us into the twenty-first century.

Electing the Scottish Parliament: Smoke-Filled Rooms or Greater Democracy?

Charles Haggerty

'The Convention is resolute that Scotland must have a parliament whose membership reflects the regional diversity of its communities; one in which men and women are fairly represented in numbers broadly proportionate to their shares of the population, and one which actively encourages the participation and involvement of all groups, including ethnic minorities, in its consultation process.'[1]

'[T]hese proposals are an alien system of government. What is remotely home-grown or Scottish about them?'[2]

Introduction

Since the inception of the Scottish Constitutional Convention[3] in July 1988, its members have been united in seeking to achieve a form of Home Rule for Scotland, and in doing so to devise a system of government for Scotland which moves away from the Westminster model. Among the SCC's many recommendations contained in its final report, Scotland's Parliament: Scotland's Right, are proposals to alter the present arrangements for electing the members of the Scottish Parliament, which are allied with other proposals to achieve sexual parity among the members of the new Parliament. By seeking to amend electoral law as it would relate to a devolved parliament, the SCC followed the precedent created by the Royal Commission on the Constitution in 1973, which recommended the use of a proportional electoral system for the devolved Assemblies then mooted for Scotland and Wales.[4] The issue has now attracted the attention of the Scottish media, who have begun to speculate on

---

[1] Scotland's Parliament: Scotland's Right. Report by the Scottish Constitutional Convention to the People of Scotland, 30th November 1995, p 21.

[2] Michael Forsyth, MP, Secretary of State for Scotland, in his Richard Stewart Memorial Lecture delivered at the University of Strathclyde on 30th November 1995: the same day as the launch of Scotland's Parliament: Scotland's Right in Edinburgh.

[3] Hereinafter 'the SCC' or 'the Convention'.

[4] Report of the Royal Commission on the Constitution (The Kilbrandon Report), Cmnd 5460, paras 779–788.

the composition of the first Scottish Parliament.[5] Should the next United
Kingdom General Election result in either a Labour administration or a
Labour and Liberal Democrat coalition, these proposals will be implemented,
assuming that the new Government is able to pilot its devolution Bill through
the Commons and a possibly hostile House of Lords. The proponents of
change argue that it will lead to democratic renewal, first for Scotland and
ultimately for the rest of the United Kingdom. Those against warn that the
proposals would mean weak coalition government, with the smaller parties
playing the role of 'kingmaker', and democracy reduced to little more than
party members being appointed as representatives of the people behind closed
doors in 'smoke-filled rooms'. This paper examines the electoral system which
is proposed for the Scottish Parliament, the ways in which it differs from the
present system, and the difficulties there may be in implementing the plans for
a devolved Parliament which is subordinate to Westminster.

The Westminster system

At present, elections for the United Kingdom Parliament, and for most other
levels of government in the United Kingdom, are conducted under the first-
past-the-post,[6] or relative majority system. For parliamentary elections the
system in essence operates as follows. The country is divided into a number of
single-member constituencies – 651 at present, although this will rise to 659 at
the next election. Those – usually nominees of constituency parties – who
satisfy the basic statutory requirements may stand for election in these
constituencies.[7] Candidates are also required to lodge a £500 deposit, which is
forfeited if they do not receive more than 5 per cent of the votes cast in the
constituency. Electors are presented with a simple choice between the various
candidates standing in the constituency in which they vote. Each elector has a
single vote and is expected to indicate a preference for one candidate only on
the ballot paper. At the close of the ballot, the votes are counted in each
constituency, and the eventual winner is the candidate who receives the most
votes. Under the FPTP system there are no prizes for coming second. The

---

[5] See 'Queue for Calton Hill', *Scotland on Sunday*, 19th January 1997. Using 'inside information
and informed speculation' the newspaper predicted that the composition of a first Scottish
Parliament would be as follows: Scottish Labour Party 51 seats, Scottish Liberal Democrats 16
seats, Scottish Conservatives 30 seats, SNP 28 seats, and Scottish Socialist Alliance, Shetland
Movement and Scottish Greens 1 seat each. This outcome was arrived at by using the 1992
General Election returns and applying the electoral scheme proposed by the SCC to them.

[6] Hereinafter 'FPTP'.

[7] These include the following: that the candidate is over twenty-one years of age; that he or she is
properly nominated and seconded by electors living in the constituency; and that to the best of
his or her knowledge the candidate is not subject to any disqualification, either under the House
of Commons (Disqualification) Act 1975 or in common law.

successful candidate is simply the one with more votes – even just one more vote – than any of the other candidates.

To illustrate this let us examine the 1992 General Election result in the Inverness, Nairn and Lochaber constituency.

Inverness, Nairn and Lochaber 1992 General Election Result	
Sir Russell Johnston (*Lib Dem*)	13,258
David Stewart (*Lab*)	12,800
Fergus Ewing (*SNP*)	12,562
John Scott (*Con*)	11,517

It can be clearly seen that only 1,741 votes separate the winner, the Liberal Democrat candidate, from the fourth-place Conservative candidate. Crucially, a majority of the voting electorate in that particular constituency – almost 74 per cent of those who voted – did not vote for the person who was elected. This highlights a major fault in the FPTP system: a large number of the electorate in a constituency can be *de facto* disenfranchised, their votes being wasted if they cast them for any candidate other than the one who triumphs. Supporters of FPTP argue that it is a relatively simple system, the mechanics of which the electorate can understand, and because it normally provides large parliamentary majorities for the winning party it ensures that there is a strong and stable Government in the country. These features, they argue, are in direct contrast to other electoral systems which incorporate an element of proportionality.

Critics of the present FPTP system point to the lack of consensus politics, which is the product of government having artificially large majorities, and to the lack of proportionality in seats gained for votes won which distorts the public support for the two principal parties in the country. This can be seen by an analysis of the 1983 General Election result.

1983 General Election Result[8]			
Party	*Seats gained in Commons*	*Percentage of seats gained*	*Percentage share of votes*
Conservative	397	61	42.4
Labour	209	32	27.6
Alliance	23	3.5	25.4

As can easily be deduced, there was no element of proportionality in the 1983 election, with the two principal parties being the beneficiaries under this

---

[8] House of Commons Information Office Factsheet No 22, General Election Results 9th June 1983.

system, and the Alliance being the greatest loser. This can be attributed to the basis of the FPTP system being the single-member constituency where 'the winner takes all'. This tends to favour those parties with a strong socio-economic base in particular regions, being mainly the Conservative and Labour Parties, while discriminating against those with a geographically widespread support throughout the country. In fact, there has not been a Government in the United Kingdom which has won a majority of the vote in the country since the end of the Second World War, and on more than one occasion the administration has been formed by a party which received a smaller percentage of the vote but a larger number of seats than its nearest rival.[9]

However, contrary to widely held belief, the FPTP system is not the only one which is used, or has been used, in the United Kingdom. In Northern Ireland the single transferable vote system has been in use for elections to the European Parliament since 1978, and was also used to elect MPs from the old University Constituencies in the United Kingdom between 1918 and 1948.[10] Indeed, the present Conservative Government – the arch-critics of the SCC proposals – have published proposals for a new Northern Ireland Assembly, elections to which are to be conducted under a form of proportional representation, and have also recently used a complicated electoral procedure involving multi-member constituencies, electoral quotas and party lists, for elections to the Northern Ireland Peace Forum.[11]

The Convention consensus on an electoral system

The SCC's disenchantment with the United Kingdom electoral system was evident from an early stage, and was patently clear in its early reports which presented the criteria for the fairer electoral arrangements which it sought.[12] Perhaps it was because of their experience of the vagaries of FPTP, com-

---

[9] The highest percentage of the vote received by a party in a post-war General Election was the 49.7% achieved by the Conservatives in 1955. In the February 1974 General Election, the Labour Party assumed power with 301 seats from 37.1% of the vote, whereas the Conservatives received 37.9% of the vote but obtained only 297 seats. There was a similar outcome after the 1951 General Election, though then the vagaries of FPTP favoured the Conservatives.

[10] The single transferable vote (hereinafter 'STV') is a complicated electoral system which operates using large multi-member constituencies, multiple-preference votes, and an electoral formula which is used to calculate a quota of votes which the winning candidates have to achieve.

[11] Frameworks for the Future (HMSO, 1995). See also the Northern Ireland (Entry to Negotiations, etc) Act 1996.

[12] These are as follows: proportionality between seats and votes; achieving stable government; giving each MSP an exclusive link with a geographical area; enabling the maximum number of votes to count towards the election of MSPs; obtaining fair representation for women and ethnic minorities; giving representation to minority parties; giving voters maximum choice over who is elected; and having a system that is easy to use and understand. See Towards a Scottish Parliament, SCC, October 1989, p 57.

pounded by seventeen years in opposition, that led the principal political parties to the SCC – Labour and the Liberal Democrats – to choose to adopt a different system for election to the Scottish Parliament than has been used for elections to the United Kingdom Parliament. Central to their thinking lay an insistence on the inclusion of an element of proportionality, though tensions arose in seeking agreement on the degree of proportionality. Ideally the Liberals would have chosen a form of STV which would have given purely proportional results, while some in the Labour Party wished to minimise the proportionality of the system chosen. The two parties eventually reached an agreement that the alternative member system[13] should be used, which is the voting system used in Germany.

AMS would operate for Scotland as follows. The country would still be divided up into the present parliamentary constituencies, returning seventy-three Members of the Scottish Parliament.[14] This total would consist of one member from each of the seventy-two Westminster constituencies, with an additional MSP for the constituency of Orkney and the Shetlands, each of whom would elect one MSP. Each party would also put forward a separate list of candidates for a specified number of additional seats. The electorate would thus have two votes: one for a constituency MSP and one for a party list. The constituency MSP would be elected under the FPTP system, but the elector would also cast a second vote for the party of his or her choice. These second votes would then be used to allocate the additional seats in proportion to the number required to ensure proportional representation. There would be nothing to prevent an elector from voting for a candidate of one party as the constituency MSP and voting for a different party on the party list.

The AMS system favoured by the SCC differs in some respects from that operated in Germany. A minimum threshold is required in elections to the Bundestag, which in practice means that for a party to have members elected from its list it must achieve either 5 per cent of the list vote or, alternatively, have three constituency members returned. This threshold is designed to prevent a proliferation of small extremist parties from gaining representation in the Bundestag. There is no equivalent proposal in Scotland's Parliament: Scotland's Right, and neither is there any mention of the retention of candidates' deposits.

One method for the proportional allocation of the votes on the party list is to apply the d'Hondt rule – a mechanism designed to ensure that the number of votes which elect each party list member are as equal as possible for all the

---

[13] Hereinafter 'AMS'.
[14] Hereinafter 'MSPs'.

parties.[15] It thus seeks to equalise the votes cast for a party and the number of seats which it obtains. The following simple example of votes in a six-member constituency illustrates the operation of this mechanism.

	Party 1	**Party 2**	**Party 3**
Votes received	420	380	200

Clearly Party 1 receives the first seat because it has the largest number of votes. However, it should not win the second because this would mean that Party 1 would have a seat for every 210 votes, while Party 2 has no seat for 380 votes. Party 2 must therefore receive the second seat, and the mechanism continues to operate in this way.

	Party 1	**Party 2**	**Party 3**
Votes received	420 (1st seat)	380 (2nd seat)	200 (4th seat)
Dividing by 2	210 (3rd seat)	190 (5th seat)	100
Dividing by 3	140 (6th seat)	126	

The last underlined figure is called the d'Hondt quota and is the number of votes that a party must receive to have a seat from the list. The result is that the number of wasted votes is minimised.

Advocates of the AMS system point to the element of proportionality inherent in it while still maintaining MSP links with individual constituencies, which is a strong positive feature of FPTP.

The parties to the SCC agreed that the party list seats would be divided up between the eight Scottish constituencies for elections to the European Parliament.[16] The question that remained was how many seats were to be allocated to each of these constituencies. The Liberal Democrats wanted a Parliament with a total of 145 members, composed of the seventy-three constituency MSPs plus nine for each of the eight European Parliamentary constituencies, which would be one for each of the Westminster constituencies

---

[15] The d'Hondt rule was used in Germany to allocate party list seats, though from 1987 Germany has operated the Hare-Niemyer system. This operates by dividing the total national vote by the number of seats to be allocated to establish a quota. Each party's vote is then divided by the quota, with seats allocated accordingly. If any seats are not filled they go to the parties with the largest number of remaining votes. (Paul Wilder, 1991). See further, Enid Lakeman, Twelve Democracies: The Electoral Systems in the European Community.

[16] These are Glasgow, North East Scotland, Mid-Scotland and Fife, Highlands and Islands, Lothian, South of Scotland, Strathclyde East, and Strathclyde West.

contained in a European Parliamentary constituency in Scotland. The rationale was that the greater the number of party list seats, the greater the possibility that this 'would produce a greater proportionality in the result of any election. Indeed, such numbers would produce a level of proportionality in the result at least equal to that of STV'.[17] The Labour Party was less enthusiastic about this degree of proportionality, and sought a Parliament composed of 112 members – seventy-two elected under FPTP and forty elected by the party list votes in the European Parliamentary constituencies.[18] Eventually a compromise was reached for a 129-seat Parliament, with seventy-three constituency MSPs elected by FPTP, and fifty-six elected from party lists, seven MSPs for each European Parliamentary constituency.

The political bargaining which took place while formulating the exact AMS proposals had a rationale. As can be seen above, the Liberal Democrats wanted more party list MSPs as this would give a higher degree of proportionality in the final-votes-cast-to-seats-obtained analysis and improve representation for the smaller parties. It would also increase the likelihood of no party having an overall majority in the Scottish Parliament, thereby leading to the prospect of a coalition Government and consensus politics. Labour wanted fewer party list MSPs for the opposite reasons – reducing the degree of proportionality and giving it a greater opportunity to obtain outright control of the Scottish Parliament.

Projected results using AMS

The likely outcome of a Scottish General Election using the AMS system proposed by the SCC is impossible to predict with any certainty for a number of reasons. There is the intangible that the first election to the Scottish Parliament would probably take place in the middle of the five-year term of the Labour administration, a period when the incumbent Government is normally at its least popular with the electorate. There is also uncertainty as to the extent to which the electorate might choose to vote for a candidate from one party as their constituency MSP and another party on the party list. However, some indication of the possible outcome is to apply the most recent electoral measures of Scottish public opinion – the 1992 General Election and 1995 local government election – on the assumption that the elector will choose to vote for the same party in the constituency vote and the party list vote.

---

[17] Unlocking the Potential: The Final Steps Towards the Completion of the Scottish Constitutional Convention's Scheme for a Scottish Parliament, Scottish Liberal Democrats, April 1995, p 6.

[18] This was prior to the agreement for separate representation for the Orkney and Shetland Isles. It envisaged five MSPs being returned from each European Parliament constituency.

1992 General Election Results in Scotland		
Party	*Percentage vote*	*Seats in the House of Commons*
Labour	39	49
Lib Dem	13	10
Conservative	26	11
SNP	21	3

Projected Outcome Using AMS for Scottish Parliament Elections		
Party	*Percentage vote*	*Seats (constituency + list)*
Labour	39	50 (49 + 1)
Lib Dem	13	17 (10 + 7)
Conservative	26	34 (11 + 23)
SNP	21	27 (3 + 24)
Independent	1	1 (0 + 1)

1995 Scottish Local Government Election Results[19]		
Party	*Percentage vote*	*Projected seats in Scottish Parliament*
Labour	44	57
Lib Dem	10	13
Conservative	11	14
SNP	27	35
Independent	7	10

These projections make for interesting reading. With an absolute majority in the Parliament being sixty-five seats, it can be seen that no one party would have overall control, leading to the likelihood of a coalition Government and the anticipated consensus politics. It can reasonably be assumed that the SCC partners, Labour and Liberal Democrat, would form a coalition, for the lifetime of the first Parliament at least. From the 1995 figures, there is the much less likely possibility of a three-party coalition which did not involve the Labour Party. However, this would require the Conservative Party and SNP to work together – something that may prove to be well nigh impossible.

A further consideration is whether there will be a difference in the political standing of constituency MSPs and MSPs elected on the party list. Obviously, MSPs will formally be of the same status for the purposes of parliamentary functions and procedure. However, it does not necessarily follow that the two categories of MSP will enjoy the same political status. It is, for instance,

[19] Although wards for local government elections are contained within parliamentary constituencies, it is difficult to illustrate the constituency/list breakdown in this projection. Consequently these can be no more than cautious predictions.

conceivable that constituency MSPs may have a relatively greater political authority.

Gender balance

In addition to altering the way in which MSPs are to be elected, the SCC also seeks, as far as possible, to achieve gender balance in the new Parliament. According to the SCC, 'Locally and nationally, women have been persistently under-represented in all areas of public life in Scotland. We believe that a new Scottish Parliament is a greater opportunity to improve radically the representation of women in Scottish politics.'[20] To symbolise this commitment the Convention ratified the Electoral Agreement, which had been drawn up by the two principal political parties to the SCC.[21] This states that the parties

'formally agree to accept the principle that there should be an equal number of men and women as members of the first Scottish Parliament. In order to achieve this aim the parties agree and commit themselves to:
- select and field an equal number of male and female candidates for election, taking into account the constituency and Additional Member List candidates.
- ensure that these candidates are equally distributed with a view to the winnability of seats'.[22]

These are laudable aims, for which the two parties should be congratulated. There are, however, problems which may arise in their implementation.

Much may depend on what the status of the Electoral Agreement is at the time of the elections to a Scottish Parliament. It has to be recognised that at present the Agreement is simply an agreement between two political parties. There are no legal sanctions should either party decide not to implement it, though there could be serious political repercussions for those who breach it. It also has to be recognised that it is simply an agreement and only two of the political parties who are likely to contest elections to the Scottish Parliament have agreed to abide by it. The Conservatives and the SNP, who are not parties to the SCC, are also not party to the Agreement, and are under no obligation whatsoever to implement it. In the event that the new Government at Westminster incorporated elements of the Agreement in primary legislation, circumstances would obviously be different. This is unlikely, unless prior preparatory work has begun, because substantial analysis would be required to determine the impact of the Agreement on the first election to a Scottish Parliament – an election which will have many other electoral imponderables.

If the Agreement is not to be given statutory force, the question is how is it

---

[20] Scotland's Parliament: Scotland's Right, p 22.
[21] The Electoral Agreement was drawn up on 23rd November 1995 and signed by the leaders of the Scottish Labour Party and Scottish Liberal Democrats, George Robertson, MP and Jim Wallace, MP, and the Chairs of the Parties, Rhona Brankin and Marilyne MacLaren.
[22] The Electoral Agreement is reproduced in Scotland's Parliament: Scotland's Right, p 23.

to be implemented in practice. Political parties, at least those who have signed the Agreement, may seek to impose all-male and all-female short lists for constituencies, and ensure that they are distributed equally among safe and target seats. In addition to the fact that this would probably not be adopted by the political parties which are not party to the Agreement, there are legal problems in such a policy. In 1993, the Labour Party in the United Kingdom introduced an arrangement whereby all-female short lists were drawn up for selection as official party candidates in 50 per cent of certain constituencies. This was challenged before an industrial tribunal by two male Labour party members who were not considered for seats which had been allocated for all-female short lists. As such, they claimed that they had been discriminated against by being rejected for consideration because they were male.[23] In finding for the applicants and against the Labour Party, the industrial tribunal unanimously held that the Sex Discrimination Act 1975 was broad enough to cover 'all kinds of professions, vocations, occupations, and trades ... including thereby persons who hold public office'. Members of Parliament come into the last category because they are 'engaged in an occupation which involves public service and for which they receive remuneration from public funds'.[24] In reaching this conclusion the tribunal recognised that although organisations may 'advance that aim by positive action, they are precluded by UK law from doing so by positive discrimination'.[25] The Labour Party did not appeal against the decision, which perhaps indicates that it accepted that its scheme, although meritorious, was unlawful. Consequently, it is likely that any such scheme which sought to achieve gender balance in candidates for election to a Scottish Parliament would be similarly unlawful, unless of course it were given a legislative basis.

Reviewing the electoral system

There remains the question of what mechanism there will be to review the electoral system for elections to the Scottish Parliament. In the United Kingdom, review of the parliamentary electoral system has been undertaken by Speakers' Conferences,[26] the Boundary Commissions and Royal Commissions. The SCC recognises that the Scottish Parliament initially 'will be dependent on boundaries established for the Westminster and European Parliaments' and that '[t]hese may be subject to alteration outwith the control of Scotland's

---

[23] *Jepson and Dyas-Elliot* v *The Labour Party* [1996] IRLR 116.
[24] Ibid at p 118.
[25] Ibid at p 117.
[26] A Speaker's Conference is a device occasionally used to discuss electoral reform. The party leaders meet privately with the Speaker of the Commons in an attempt to secure all-party support for proposed changes.

Parliament, and it will be necessary to ensure that separate boundary reviews for the Parliament can be carried out with the purpose of maintaining the size of the Parliament and the integrity of the corrective effect of the additional members. This function will be carried out by the Boundary Commission for Scotland'.[27]

In addition to this, the SCC recognises that the novelty and uniqueness of its proposed AMS system requires that the Scottish Parliament 'should conduct an enquiry after the first election and periodically thereafter ... to establish its success in fulfilling the objectives of the Convention'. The SCC ends by declaring that the electoral system should 'not be easily challenged or changed without careful and democratic scrutiny' and that 'a mechanism should therefore be devised so that technical and corrective changes in the Parliament, as agreed by the Parliament itself, can be carried through without undue delay'.[28]

The fulfilment of these objectives turns on the extent of the legislative competence of the Scottish Parliament with respect to electoral law, whether such competence is capable of entrenchment and the means of resolving disputes over the scope and exercise of the competence. These are matters which, in a broader context, are addressed in the papers of Jean McFadden and William Bain and of Colin Boyd. However, it is appropriate here to explore the narrower issue of the options available in allocating legislative competence over electoral law.

On the assumption that the proposals of the SCC are adopted, powers will be devolved in a reserved manner. The United Kingdom Parliament will maintain certain specified functions, and the remainder will be, in the language of the Convention, 'sole or shared' powers.[29] The question is, where will electoral law lie?

Electoral law as a sole power

This arrangement would leave the Scottish Parliament with sole authority to amend the law regulating the manner in which it was elected. There would be an obvious conflict of interest in the arrangement – there being no apparent check or balance on the exercise of such a fundamental power. The dangers can be illustrated by examining the analogous situation which existed in

---

[27] Scotland's Parliament: Scotland's Right, pp 21–22.

[28] Ibid at p 22.

[29] Scotland's Parliament: Scotland's Right, p 12. The main powers to be retained at the centre are listed there as defence, foreign affairs, immigration and nationality, social security and central economic and fiscal policies. This is the method which was employed to devolve powers to Stormont by the Government of Ireland Act 1920. The Constitution Unit in its report, Scotland's Parliament: Fundamentals for a New Scotland Act, also advocates this method of transferring power.

Ireland. The Government of Ireland Act 1920, s 4(1), gave Stormont the power
'to make laws for the peace, order and good government ... of Northern
Ireland', subject to a list of matters specifically reserved to Westminster. The
devolved powers included, in s 14(5), the power to alter the procedure for
elections to Stormont.[30] The 1920 Act had incorporated a system of proportional representation for these elections which was used for the elections in
1921 and 1925. However, the Unionist-dominated Parliament exercised its
powers under s 14(5), and in 1929 successfully introduced a bill to replace
proportional representation with FPTP.[31] This was apparently done without
consultation beyond Unionist circles. This demonstrates the inherent dangers,
but it is not to suggest that they are as likely to be faced in Scotland.

Scotland is not beset by the problems which have plagued Northern Ireland.
Also, under the proposed AMS system of elections to the Scottish Parliament it
is unlikely that a single party would win such a majority of the seats that it
would be able to dominate the proceedings of the Scottish Parliament as the
Unionists were able to dominate proceedings in Stormont.

Electoral law as a reserved power

By this arrangement Westminster would retain exclusive legislative competence with respect to the regulation of elections to the Scottish Parliament,
which, in its absolute form, entails no statutory duty to consult the Scottish
people or the Scottish Parliament, although such a duty could be incorporated
in the devolution legislation. This would have attractions for those who wish to
emphasise the subordinate status of the Scottish Parliament, but for some it
would create problems for its constitutional and political legitimacy. The
arrangement would also be capable of exacerbating constitutional instability
and political tension were a Government in Westminster and a Government in
Scotland to pursue radically divergent policies.

Electoral law as a shared responsibility

Making legislative competence in respect of electoral law a shared power
between the United Kingdom Parliament and the Scottish Parliament may be
both a practical solution and a solution to be preferred. The SCC has already
indicated that it envisages a role for the Boundary Commission for Scotland in
reviewing and redefining the constituencies for elections to the Scottish
Parliament, and that it also wishes to review the operation of the system itself

---

[30] Section 14(5) provided: 'After three years from the day of the first meeting of the Parliament of
Northern Ireland that Parliament may alter the qualification and registration of the electors, the
law relating to elections ... the constituencies, and the distribution of members among the
constituencies. ...'

[31] House of Commons (Methods of Voting and Redistribution) Act (NI) 1929.

to ascertain whether it is fulfilling its criteria for a better electoral system. The Commission is a body regulated by the Parliamentary Constituencies Act 1986, which is composed of the Speaker of the House of Commons, a senior judge and two other members, who are appointed by the United Kingdom Government. Its function is to provide a review every twelve years of the constituencies within its geographical remit. In Scotland the functions and membership of the Boundary Commission could be amended when reviewing the electoral constituencies for the Scottish Parliament to take into account the unique electoral provisions north of the border, and also to admit appointees of the Scottish Parliament, giving it added legitimacy. Ideally this would include senior members of the Scottish Parliament, such as the Speaker. The functions could conceivably be expanded to empower it to examine the whole area of electoral law and not just constituency boundaries, thus avoiding two inquiries being carried out by different bodies, with the potential for overlap and conflict. It would have the power to report to both Parliaments with its recommendations. For these to become law the approval of both Parliaments will be required, and in Scotland there may also be a case for including some pre-legislative referendum procedure. If this were considered too great an expansion of the powers and duties of the Boundary Commission for Scotland, an alternative may be to develop both the competence of the Commission and, in a parallel manner, the Speaker's Conference.

Conclusions

In developing proposals for establishing the Scottish Parliament the SCC was obliged to achieve a delicate equilibrium in finding a distinctive and more representative arrangement for the elections to an institution which would continue to function within the United Kingdom. It is perhaps not surprising that the outcome has its legal and constitutional uncertainties as well as its political critics who view legislative and executive devolution to Scotland itself with some suspicion.

Nevertheless, leaving behind the shackles of tradition, the SCC has agreed a new and fair electoral system which is inclusive and not, like FPTP, exclusive in nature. It is clear that the SCC seeks to establish the legitimacy of the Scottish Parliament in the eyes of the Scottish people, thus reducing the possibility of its abolition by a hostile Westminster. The new electoral system, despite the attendant difficulties discussed here, is intended as one element of that legitimacy.

Devolution and the Scottish Legal Institutions

Gordon Jackson, QC

Introduction

Any devolved parliament will, in carrying out its functions, have a large impact on the areas of law and justice within Scotland. To state that may seem to be stating the obvious as the legal system in Scotland is already to a large degree separate and different from that in the rest of the United Kingdom. It may be thought, therefore, that this is one area in which the change is less far reaching and that it is no real change at all. Devolution in this area at least may be seen as merely maintaining the status quo to a considerable extent.

The 1978 Act, however, was not entirely clear in this regard. An examination of the devolved powers in Part 1 of Sched 10 and the reserved matters in Part 2 reveal a degree of ambiguity and might suggest that the devolving of the legal system was half hearted at best, as power which at first sight may seem to be devolved under Part 1 is then reserved under Part 2. The present proposals, and in particular those of the Scottish Constitutional Convention, go much further and if followed will mean that, in general terms, the Scottish Parliament will have far greater responsibility for the legal system than was formerly envisaged.

This is to be welcomed but it would be a mistake to conclude that this is now one area in which no real planning is necessary as no problems are likely to arise. The legislation of the United Kingdom Parliament will still deal with certain matters on a national basis and difficulties will inevitably arise. To have two separate legal systems administered and controlled at any one time by the one government is one thing. To have two systems under two separate governments, each with legislative power, is quite another. This is a very significant change which will be seen both in the way the law itself develops and in the structure and control of the legal institutions. It is therefore necessary before establishing a devolved parliament to be aware of the effect of such a change and how that might best be dealt with in order to achieve the twin objectives of devolving real power while safeguarding the basic unity of the United Kingdom.

This paper is simply an attempt at least to identify some of the matters which may require further thought. On occasions solutions are offered in order to suggest possible ways ahead. Some of them may well be open to legitimate criticism, but the fact that any proposed idea is different from how things have been done in the past, particularly at Westminster, should not of itself be any barrier whatsoever. For many years there has been within Scotland a real vision for a Scottish assembly. That is not, however, an end in itself. The criticism is often made that a Scottish Parliament will be no more than the old Strathclyde Regional Council on a bigger scale. It will not be. On the other hand it does not need to be Westminster in miniature. What is needed is a parliament within Scotland which is able to meet the demands of its own society and time. That may require us to think about our existing institutions in a new way.

Legislative power

It is clear that the devolved parliament will have the power to change the law, including the criminal law, insofar as that is not related to a reserved power. This will mean that the Scottish Parliament will regulate not only criminal procedure but a large part of the substantive criminal law. Although this is an obvious result of any real devolution of power, it may have far-reaching consequences.

At present there are a great many procedural differences between the system in Scotland and elsewhere but the substantive law tends to remain broadly similar in its general approach. This is only to be expected when the same government is legislating for both systems at any one time. When that changes there will be the potential for substantial differences to develop over a period of time and the possibility for the two systems to go in quite different directions. This must be anticipated. One example, albeit an extreme one, will illustrate the point. There may again be a debate about the reintroduction of capital punishment. What if one parliament votes for its return while the other remains resolutely against? Would that be acceptable? Could the Union survive if there was that degree of difference? That, in my opinion, must be doubtful. Such a divergence may be legally possible and does occur in, for example, the United States. That, however, is in the context of a long-established federal system. We have a different history and culture and it is difficult to imagine the United Kingdom maintaining its unity with that degree of difference.

That, it might be argued, is extreme and fanciful. There may even be other and better examples of where substantial divergence is likely to occur. Perhaps so, but this does serve to illustrate the basic and serious problem. When two parliaments legislate there is the possibility, if not the likelihood, of their going in quite different directions. Such differences may only reflect the different attitudes which are inevitable between any two areas, but when they are enshrined within two separate legal systems that divergence becomes very apparent and it thereby becomes clear that the two countries are moving in quite different directions. If there is a considerable divergence, not only in procedure but in substance and principles, that may undermine the basic unity of the United Kingdom in a very significant way.

How then is such a danger to be avoided? On one view the answer is simple. The United Kingdom Parliament will remain the sovereign legislature and be able, therefore, to control the situation by its own legislation. Indeed, according to the traditional view of sovereignty – as explained in the paper by Jean McFadden and William Bain – such a situation is inevitable as the sovereign United Kingdom Parliament will always be able to legislate on any matter, including those devolved to the Scottish Parliament.

It may, however, not be quite as simple as that. It may be unacceptable, politically if not legally, for the Scottish Parliament to have devolved power which can, in reality, be countermanded at will by Westminster. On one view that is no real devolution at all and that may, at least in the longer term, be unacceptable to the Scottish people.

A better solution may be to put within the devolution legislation limits on the legislative competence of both parliaments by expressly stating that only the Scottish Parliament can legislate on devolved matters. The potential divergence would then be countered by placing a constitutional limit on the legislative power of all parliaments within the United Kingdom, including Westminster. This would require something in the nature of a Bill of Rights which would enshrine basic and fundamental principles within the United Kingdom as a whole so that no parliament would be able to legislate contrary to that.

It is appreciated that such an approach raises difficult questions, both legally and politically. It can be argued that, in the light of the doctrine of parliamentary sovereignty, such provisions are worthless and therefore to be avoided. I do not accept that. The traditional view of sovereignty is not as straight forward as is often suggested. In any event the inclusion of such provisions would have a real political effect. Indeed the cynic might suspect that the unwillingness to include any such provisions owes as much to the political desire to limit the power of a devolved parliament as to any real legal objection.

In any event the problem will have to be considered with some care. Of course there are theoretical difficulties. Undoubtedly any such provisions will require to be drafted with very great care. Nevertheless the objective must be to establish a devolved parliament with real power while avoiding a divergence which might undermine the Union. This may not be a problem in the short term but the task is to create a structure able to survive time and change. This is a major alteration to the political structure of the United Kingdom and will need to be approached with an attitude of mind that is prepared to re-examine long-established positions and find appropriate solutions to these new problems.

The Lord Advocate
The office of the Lord Advocate is central to the legal system within Scotland. Not only does the holder of that office exercise considerable direct power and influence but any changes within the legal institutions, such as the creation of a Ministry of Justice, are likely to have an effect on the role of the Lord Advocate. Any consideration of how the legal institutions will operate under a devolved parliament must therefore begin with an examination of the Lord Advocate's own position.

In the 1978 Act the role of the Lord Advocate was not clearly defined. Section 20(6) stated:

> 'A Scottish Secretary or assistant to a Scottish Secretary who is to perform functions corresponding to functions performed by a Law Officer of the Crown may (whether or not he is to perform also other functions) be appointed notwithstanding that he is not a member of the Assembly, and may then take part in the proceedings of the Assembly but shall not vote.'

The inference from this is that the office of Lord Advocate would remain as part of the United Kingdom Government although certain functions presently performed by him would be devolved.

This is no longer acceptable and the office of Lord Advocate should itself be devolved, with the Lord Advocate being appointed by the devolved government and answerable to the devolved parliament. There are a number of reasons why that would be appropriate.

First, the present devolution proposals advocate that the legal system be devolved to a much fuller extent than in 1978, both in terms of the courts and the prosecution of crime. Although problems will still arise, it is at least now clear that the devolved parliament will have responsibility for the greater part of the functions presently performed by the Lord Advocate. In that situation it would make no sense to retain the office as part of the United Kingdom Government.

Secondly, the office of Lord Advocate is an ancient one. The line of Lord Advocates can be traced back to 1483 and the office thus ante-dates the Union of the Crowns, the Union of 1707 and even the establishment of the Court of Session in 1532. The Lord Advocate was therefore recognised as an important

Officer of State well before the Union of 1707 and indeed was an ex-officio member of the pre-1707 Scottish Parliament. The office has no exact English counterpart and as a distinctive Scottish institution emphasises continuity within Scotland down the centuries. It is thus entirely appropriate that when Scotland again has its own legislative body the Lord Advocate should be a member of that assembly, whether as an elected member or on an ex-officio basis. This would also mean that the Lord Advocate could answer directly to the Scottish Parliament insofar as that is appropriate. At present during Scottish questions at Westminster the last ten minutes are when questions to the Lord Advocate are taken, but in recent years the reality has often been that the response must come from someone other than a law officer. This is unsatisfactory and would be avoided by the present proposals.

Against this background it is necessary to consider briefly what the functions of the Lord Advocate would be within a devolved government and in particular how they would differ, if at all, from the present position.

The prosecution system

It is appropriate that the prosecution system should be devolved. The 1978 Act did not do that but the present proposals of the Scottish Constitutional Convention go much further in general terms and although they do not specifically mention the prosecution system it would be anomalous in the extreme to devolve the legal system in the terms now suggested but exclude the prosecution system.

At present the Lord Advocate is in charge of the system of prosecution and should continue to exercise this function within a Scottish Government. It has however been suggested that this is an opportunity to reconsider the whole matter on the basis that there is an argument that the head of the prosecution system should not be a member of the government. The argument for this seems to be that this may give rise to a conflict of interest which would be against the proper interests of justice.

The reality, however, is that although such a danger may exist in theory, the present system works well in practice. Lord Advocates appointed by governments of differing political hues have, over many years, been well able to administer the system of prosecution in an entirely appropriate manner. There is therefore no need to make any change to the present system. That having been said, it is appropriate to emphasise at this time of change that the Lord Advocate must remain able to perform this function totally impartially and free from all political interference, and that being a member of both the devolved government and parliament must not be allowed to undermine that in any way.

It is however necessary in this context to face up to another problem which will arise. There will be areas of law which will not be devolved and which will give rise to criminal prosecutions. Examples may be offences under the Misuse of Drugs Act 1971 or the Companies Acts, or in connection with any matter which will continue to be dealt with on a United Kingdom basis to ensure a uniform approach. In such a situation, how are prosecutions to be undertaken? If it is to be at the instance of the Lord Advocate, that will mean that he will be ordering and conducting prosecutions on matters which are within the legislative competence of a parliament to which he is not responsible (either directly or as a member of the government which is responsible to that parliament) and in which he does not sit. This has at least the potential to cause problems, particularly if the two governments are quite different in their politics and policies.

The alternative would seem to be to have two different prosecution systems operating within the one jurisdiction. This may be technically possible but would seem to be undesirable and liable to cause more problems that it would solve as well as causing an unnecessary increase in bureaucracy and expense.

It would appear, therefore, that the Lord Advocate should be responsible for all prosecutions within Scotland, even when the matter is within the responsibility of the United Kingdom legislature. This will demand a degree of co-operation but that should not be an insurmountable difficulty, particularly if care is taken to emphasise the independence of the Lord Advocate from all political interference on such matters.

Government legal adviser
A major part of the Lord Advocate's work is the giving of legal advice to the Government. This involves, for example, the scrutiny of proposed legislation, the drafting of legislation applicable to Scotland by way of parliamentary draftsmen in the Lord Advocate's Department in London, and giving advice and assistance to Government departments involved in civil litigation. It is clear that the Scottish Executive will also require such assistance; indeed access to legal advice of the highest calibre will be of the utmost importance to the new Executive, especially in the early days when the relationship between the United Kingdom and Scottish activities of government has to be precisely determined. This will be even more important when, as may well happen, there are different parties in government in Edinburgh and London. It has not been and will not be enough for the new Executive to rely on legally qualified civil servants for advice. The questions put to them have to be framed and the answers interpreted in the light of government policy by one committed to that policy. The repercussions of changes for other areas of law and policy have to

be foreseen. It is appropriate that the Lord Advocate should perform this role as one of the Scottish Executive ministerial team.

The effect of this is to continue the present position whereby the Lord Advocate is responsible for two quite separate operations: the prosecution of crime through the Crown Office and the provision of legal advice through the Lord Advocate's Department. There is no reason why these two functions could not continue to operate with both located in Edinburgh. The structure in the Crown Office is based on the need for that division to be maintained and this could continue in a devolved system.

Scottish law officer

A further matter will arise. The United Kingdom Government will still require to have a Scottish legal adviser as there will be many occasions when United Kingdom legislation will have a Scottish dimension. Advice will also be required when disputes arise over legislative competence, and there will be other occasions when co-operation between the two Governments and their legal advisers will be required. There will therefore be a need for a new office to be created, that of a Scottish law officer in the United Kingdom Government. This could be achieved by retaining the office of Solicitor-General in the United Kingdom structure or, preferably, by continuing to have the Solicitor-General alongside the Lord Advocate in the devolved structure and creating an entirely new office and title.

Law reform

The Scottish Constitutional Convention points out that the inefficiency of the system in legislating for Scotland has been a powerful reason for its proposals. If there has been neglect it will be up to the new parliament to rectify it, and in that respect the Lord Advocate will have a particular responsibility. At present he is responsible for law reform, particularly through the Scottish Law Commission. The members of the Commission are appointed by him and lay before him their conclusions and proposals for reform. It is clear that this relationship should continue and that the Lord Advocate should retain the responsibility for such matters and be answerable for them to the devolved parliament. This in itself emphasises the desirability of the Lord Advocate being a full member of the Scottish Parliament and therefore able to participate in the legislative process. If that were not to happen, standing orders should allow him to be called before parliament and its committees on suitable occasions.

The setting up of a parliament in Scotland will provide an opportunity to examine the whole area of continuing law reform, which may have been somewhat neglected by Westminster. As part of that exercise it would be appropriate to reconsider how a better use might be made of parliamentary committees. Under the present system there would seem to be two basic approaches: one by way of committees made up of members of parliament and taking evidence from outside parties and experts before reporting back to parliament as a whole; the other by way of committees of non-parliamentarians, such as the recent committee under the chairmanship of Professor Sutherland which looked at the system of criminal appeals and made its recommendations to parliament via the Secretary of State.

The Scottish Parliament might look at the possibility of establishing committees in a somewhat different way in order to consider various areas of the law. Such committees would take evidence and representations from interested parties on possible changes as at present but would be innovative in that they would be composed of parliamentarians and others with a particular expertise and would be able, with some weight, to make representations to parliament. The traditionalists will object to this and suggest that there are insurmountable constitutional problems in having parliamentary committees which have non-elected members. Indeed the members of the parliament may themselves be resistant to any such notion as they seek to preserve their own status.

The simple truth, however, is that the United Kingdom Parliament has lost public confidence and is seen as being more interested in political infighting than in a search for improvement in how the country is administered. A new Scottish Parliament should be genuinely responsive to the need for change. It is to be hoped that the electoral system now being proposed will itself go some way towards encouraging a less partisan approach to serious issues, and it may be that what is being suggested here will also be of assistance in that regard. Involving those with suitable expertise in this way is not to undermine the democratic process in any way whatsoever but to make it more aware of and responsive to the need for change which is part of a vibrant and progressive society.

Executive functions
There will be devolved administrative matters concerning the courts, legal aid, tribunals and legal services generally. It would be appropriate, at least pending the setting up of a Ministry of Justice, that the Lord Advocate should have ministerial responsibility for these. This yet again emphasises the need for him to be a member of the Scottish Parliament and answerable to it for his ministerial performance.

Another matter which arises is the issuing of public interest immunity certificates. At present in England these are signed by the individual Government ministers but in Scotland they are signed by the Lord Advocate, irrespective of the department involved. This latter approach could continue in connection with matters arising from the devolved government, and matters with a United Kingdom dimension coming before a Scottish court could be attended to by the Whitehall department involved or possibly by the new United Kingdom law officer dealing with Scottish matters. This is, of course, a comparatively minor issue and capable of being easily resolved, but it serves to illustrate that there are likely to be many issues of this nature which will need to be considered and dealt with if the legislation is to be effective.

Judicial appointments

The present system of appointing judges and sheriffs is shrouded in mystery. Appointments are made by the Queen acting on advice, but the precise role played by the various advisers is far from clear. What is clear is that the Lord Advocate plays an important part. In the 1970s both Scottish law officers threatened to resign when their roles in making judicial appointments appeared to be undermined, albeit that their recollections differ as to how the issue was finally resolved, which alone serves to illustrate the lack of clarity on the issue. If the statements of the present Secretary of State are to be taken at face value he seems to have a greater role than might have been thought to be the case.

The establishing of a Scottish Parliament should be seen as an opportunity to set up open procedures for judicial appointments in the form of a legal appointments commission, a body in which both the public and the legal profession could have confidence. The membership would be a matter for debate. Although it would include those who are presently involved in making such decisions, the main difference would be that appointments would be seen to have come from a representative body rather than as the result of some vague procedure with the attendant prospect of it having been influenced by the prejudice of any one individual.

The courts

It is now proposed that the administration of the Scottish courts should be entirely devolved. That was not the case in the Scotland Act 1978. Under that legislation the courts, and the legal profession, would have been devolved, but the judiciary, except in respect to their number and, in the case of sheriffs, the territorial areas in which they were to act, would not have been devolved. This division would almost certainly have produced an unwelcome and unnecessary tension.

There would seem to be no reason in practice or principle why that should be the case and the Scottish Constitutional Convention's proposals make that welcome change. Appendix 1 of Scotland's Parliament: Scotland's Right lists as matters to be devolved courts and the legal system, juries, judges, sheriffs, justices of the peace, the legal profession, legal aid, the police, prisons, and law and order.

One question remains. How are constitutional disputes to be resolved? In particular, what role will the Scottish courts have? It is generally accepted that no matter how carefully the legislation is drawn up, disputes will arise as to whether or not a piece of legislation is within the competence of a particular parliament, and the courts will be required to adjudicate. This may arise in different ways. It may, for example, be in the context of an action proceeding in court. It may arise even before the measure has passed into law when there is a dispute between the two parliaments. This subject is fully examined in Colin Boyd's paper, the conclusion being that all such disputes should be dealt with ultimately by the Judicial Committee of the Privy Council. That is also the approach of the Constitution Unit, on the basis that there is at present 'no appetite' for establishing a separate constitutional court.

There are, however, problems with that approach. Its effect would be to bypass the Scottish courts, at least in certain circumstances, and there are strong objections to that in Scotland from those who feel that, on principle, the Scottish court should always have a say in such matters. They argue that there are matters which should always be referred to a Scottish court in the first instance, with an appeal to a higher court. The advantage of this would be that the final court would at least have the benefit of Scottish judicial opinion. A possible disadvantage is that such matters will often require speedy resolution and as the final court is likely to be used more often than not it would seem unnecessary and time-wasting to go through various levels of judicial decision-making.

The best solution would be to establish a constitutional court from the outset. This would be made up of judges from all the jurisdictions in the United Kingdom – that is, from England, Scotland and Northern Ireland – either on a full- or part-time basis, and it would sit in London and elsewhere. It would be able to adjudicate quickly on matters referred to it by either government or by a court in the course of other litigation. Even the Constitution Unit envisages such a court becoming necessary in due course and there seems to be no good reason for not establishing it at an early stage. If, as has been argued earlier in this paper, there are to be provisions in the devolution legislation and in a Bill of Rights limiting the legislative power of both parliaments, there will be an increasing need for a specialist court to deal with such matters quickly and authoritatively. The very fact of establishing such a court would be seen as giving such provisions an increased legitimacy.

Ministry of Justice

There are strong reasons for suggesting that a future Scottish Government should set up a Ministry of Justice. The justice system in the broadest sense is an area of considerable importance. To many working within it, it often seems to be fragmented. The police, for example, feel that the courts take little account of their problems. Offenders are dealt with by a number of agencies including the prison service and social work departments and there seems to be a lack of co-ordination. A Ministry of Justice would provide a forum for co-ordinating all aspects of the justice system with responsibility being given to a member of the Scottish Executive for the various parts of the justice system presently dealt with by the Secretary of State. This could lead to other changes in the system as the new department developed relationships with other parts of the existing structure, including the Lord Advocate's department.

The setting up of such a ministry and its relationship with other departments would be a matter for the Government of the day to decide. It is important, however, to make one thing clear at this stage. The independence of the Lord Advocate, in terms of criminal prosecution, must not be undermined. His function is to make decisions free from political interference or pressure. Recently there has been a tendency for politicians of all parties to challenge that process and to seek explanations for decisions made. Such pressure should be resisted. If mistakes have been made that is a different matter and the Lord Advocate has to take full responsibility when that happens. He must, however, remain free from improper interference and the establishing of a Ministry of Justice must not change that.

The Secretary of State

The question arises as to whether or not the office of Secretary of State for Scottish will disappear after devolution. Any suggestion that it will tends to produce strong reaction one way or the other, and understandably so. The Secretary of State has been an important figure for many years and has, under governments of different complexions, fought hard for Scottish interests. To lose that input at Westminster and in Whitehall would seem not to be in the best interests of Scotland.

On the other hand, the functions of the Secretary of State will largely be devolved. What then is his role to be? The 1978 legislation gave the impression that he would act as a kind of viceroy, representing Westminster in Edinburgh and with power to intervene in the Scottish legislative process. As Colin Boyd points out, it may now be inappropriate for the Secretary of State to have that role, but to take it away would further diminish the responsibility of the office and make it more difficult to identify its function. On the other hand, the continued existence of the office may serve as a focus for tension between the two governments.

This may be an area where the best approach is to wait and see how matters develop. Argument at this stage may owe more to political point scoring than anything else. The reality is that many of the tasks performed by the Secretary of State will be devolved, but the United Kingdom Government will still require a minister, at some level, to deal with issues affecting Scotland: non-devolved matters such as finance and economic policy will affect Scotland a great deal and a Scottish voice in the United Kingdom Government will continue to be of considerable value. Whether or not the Secretary of State will have a Cabinet position will be a matter for the Prime Minister of the day to decide. It is, however, to be hoped that any minister with such responsibility will continue to fight for the best interests of Scotland and that, whatever structure is finally established, it will be done in such a way as to minimise conflict between the two governments and parliaments.

Conclusion

Devolution will bring about significant changes in the way Scotland is governed and it will affect our legal institutions in a variety of ways. It will be a process of devolution in a very real sense but it will also be a process of evolution. Changes must be anticipated and there must be flexibility to allow the new situation to develop. We should now be considering how these changes will work in practice and planning accordingly.

(I have been greatly helped in writing this paper by Professor Ian Willock of the University of Dundee. Ian has supplied me with much useful material, particularly on the role of the Lord Advocate, and has generously given me the benefit of his positive criticism and suggestions on the paper as a whole. He is not, however, to be taken as agreeing with it in every respect – GJ.)

Devolution and the European Union

St John Bates

Introduction

The Scottish Constitutional Convention Report, Scotland's Parliament: Scotland's Right, has a two-page appendix listing 'some of the principal areas which will fall within the powers of Scotland's Parliament'.[1] The list differs somewhat from the matters which were to be within the competence of the Scottish Assembly and the Scottish Executive under the Scotland Act 1978.[2] These lists, compiled some twenty years apart, do have one important feature in common. In both cases the majority of the proposed areas of competence to be devolved to Scottish institutions are within the legislative competence of the European Community. The European dimension, therefore, continues to be an important element in devising a constitutionally stable contemporary scheme of devolution to Scotland. Any devolution scheme must find a balance between the Community legal obligations of the United Kingdom and the freedom of Scottish institutions to exercise their devolved powers.

In striking that balance today various factors must be taken into account. The first is that the European Union has itself changed in some respects since 1978. There have been significant institutional and procedural changes affecting the manner of its policy making and its legislative process. The European Union has become more adept at relating to federal and quasi-federal member states. Much greater emphasis is now placed on regional policy and the concept of subsidiarity has been developed. There has, however, been relatively little change in the fundamental relationship between Community law and the national law of member states. Community law prevails over national law; Community regulations are directly effective in the law of member states; Community directives must be implemented by member states and this usually requires domestic legislation. Directives are certainly now drafted in more detail, but perhaps the greatest change in this area is that a member state

---

[1] Published by the Scottish Constitutional Convention, Edinburgh, in 1995; Appendix 1.
[2] Schedules 10 and 11.

which fails to implement a Community directive, or implements it inadequately or partially, may attract liability in damages.[3]

A further related factor is the extent to which institutional change and changes in political attitude within the European Union will encourage a belief that a Scottish Government can achieve a more substantial role in the Community legislative process. In considering this matter, a clearer distinction must be drawn between the constitutional roles of a Scottish Parliament and a Scottish Executive than is perhaps evident in some current political thinking.[4]

Further factors are changes in constitutional, and in particular public law, perceptions. By way of illustration, the Scotland Act 1978 contained a variety of mechanisms which empowered the United Kingdom Government to act, without recourse to the courts, where it considered that the Scottish Assembly or the Scottish Executive had legislated or acted in breach of Community obligations, a breach for which the United Kingdom as a member state would be liable in Community law. Whether it would be considered constitutionally appropriate or, given the modern scope of judicial review, even legally possible to include the exercise of such powers without recourse to the courts in a contemporary devolution scheme must be questioned.

Devolution and the Community legislative process

The essentials of the Community legislative process, which may be altered by the current inter-governmental conference, may be stated briefly for the purposes of this paper. The European Commission has the exclusive right to initiate proposed Community legislation, although both the Council of the European Union and the European Parliament have the power to request it to bring forward a legislative proposal. The Commission develops its proposals in consultation, through working groups, with member states. The draft legislation prepared by the Commission is submitted to both the European Parliament and the Council; other Community institutions, the Economic and Social Committee and the Committee of the Regions, also have an advisory role in limited areas of legislation. The European Parliament has the power both to amend legislative proposals and to block their enactment. However, it is the Council of the European Union, composed of representatives of the govern-

---

[3] Cases C-6 and 9/90, *Francovich and Bonifaci* v *Italy* [1991] ECR I – 5357; Case C-334/92, *Miret* v *Fondo de Garantia Salarial* [1993] ECR I – 6911; Joined Cases C-46/93 and C-48/93, *Brasserie du Pêcheur SA* v *Germany* and *R* v *Secretary of State for Transport, ex p Factortame Ltd* [1996] 1 CMLR 889; Case C-392/93, *R* v *HM Treasury, ex p British Telecommunications plc* [1966] 2 CMLR 217; Case C-5/94, *R* v *Ministry of Agriculture, Fisheries and Food, ex p Hedley Lomas (Ireland) Ltd* [1996] 2 CMLR 391; Joined Cases C-178/94, 179/94, C-188/194 to C-190/94, *Dillenkofer and others* v *Germany* (unreported).

[4] See, for example, the Scottish Constitutional Convention Report, Scotland's Parliament, Scotland's Right, p 16, 'Scotland's Voice in Europe'.

ments of the member states, which formally enacts the legislation, after it has been considered, sometimes over an extensive period and with many amendments, by working groups of officials from the member states and the Committee of Permanent Representatives (COREPER). The Council reaches a decision on legislation, depending on the basis of legislative competence, either by unanimity or qualified majority vote.

The most significant forms of legislation in the context of this paper are (i) regulations which, although they may require some domestic implementation such as the establishment of administrative arrangements, are effective in law in member states once they have been enacted and (ii) directives which require to be implemented in member states, usually by legislation, but may become directly effective in law in member states if they are not so implemented within the period which they prescribe.

The Community legislative process, therefore, differs from its British counterpart in that consultation prior to the drafting of legislation is institutionalised and that the Executive has *du jure* and final legislative competence. The national parliaments of member states have no formal constitutional role in the enactment of Community legislation, although they will commonly have a domestic legislative role where Community legislation requires to be implemented in member states.

Scotland has direct representation in some of the institutions involved in the Community legislative process. Eight of the Members of the European Parliament are elected from Scottish constituencies, although this number is regulated by domestic legislation and not by Community law.[5] Of the twenty-four members of the Committee of the Regions, and an equal number of alternate members, which may be proposed by the United Kingdom for appointment by the Council of Ministers,[6] five of the members, and their alternates, are proposed by the United Kingdom Government from Scotland. Again, the number proposed from Scotland is a matter for the United Kingdom Government, but United Kingdom legislation requires those proposed to be elected members of a local authority at the time of the proposal.[7] One study has suggested that the responsibility for proposing the members from Scotland on the Committee of the Regions should be devolved to the Scottish Government and that initially the five should consist of three members of the Scottish Parliament and two elected members of local authorities.[8] Other than this

---

[5] European Parliament Elections Act 1978, s 2.
[6] EC Treaty (as amended by the Treaty on European Union), art 198a.
[7] European Communities (Amendment) Act 1993, s 6.
[8] Scotland's Parliament: Fundamentals for a New Scotland Act (The Constitution Unit, London, 1996), paras 325, 327.

direct representation, the extent to which Scotland is represented elsewhere in the bodies and institutions concerned with Community legislative process is, at present, entirely a matter for the United Kingdom Government to determine, subject in some cases to the approval of the Council of the European Union or the European Parliament, or both.

The questions which will arise under a devolution scheme are what is to be the extent and manner of the involvement of a Scottish Government in the Community legislative process, and by what means a Scottish Parliament is to be able to hold a Scottish Government to account for its involvement in that legislative process.

A Scottish Government and the Community legislative process
It has been widely recognised that the European Union has had a centralising effect on the devolved powers of units in federal, quasi-federal and decentralised member states. In a Community law context, it may be that the concept of subsidiarity will eventually compensate for this. Yet, whatever its theological provenance and its status as a political aspiration, subsidiarity still remains a rather elusive legal concept and, in the short term anyway, is unlikely, as a matter of Community law, to affect national legislative competence to implement Community legislation.[9]

However, in a domestic context the constitutional arrangements in some other member states demonstrate what may be possible.[10] Article 23 of the German Constitution requires a qualified majority both in the Bundestag and in the Bundesrat (in which representatives of the Länder sit) for the transfer of competence from Germany to the Community; provides that the decision of the Bundesrat is decisive where such a transfer of legislative competence affects the exclusive legislative competence of the Länder; and also provides that Germany may be represented by a representative of the Länder in the Council of Ministers when matters affecting the legislative competence of the Länder are being discussed. In Belgium, there is a co-operation agreement between the Federal Government, the three regional and the three community Governments which provides for the composition of Belgian delegations to the Council of Ministers and regulates the negotiating strategy of the delegation and the manner in which it votes in the absence of an agreement on such strategy. In Spain, the Government has agreed to provide the autonomous

---

[9] On subsidiarity, see for example, Subsidiarity: The Challenge of Change (European Institute of Public Administration, 1991); A. Toth, 'Is Subsidiarity Justiciable?' 19 E L Rev (1994) 268.

[10] See B. Jones and M. Keating (eds), *The European Union and the Regions* (Clarendon Press, Oxford, 1995). See also C. Jeffrey, 'The German Länder and the 1996 Inter-governmental Conference' 5 *Regional and Federal Studies* (1995) 356.

regions with information on Community developments, in particular as they relate to regional policy.[11]

The present procedures for taking account of distinctive Scottish interests in the United Kingdom negotiating position within the Community legislative process are largely contained in Whitehall arrangements. Overall responsibility for formal communication between the European Commission and the United Kingdom Government rests with the European Secretariat in the Cabinet Office, which allocates a Whitehall department as the lead department on each Commission initiative, with a responsibility to consult other relevant Whitehall departments. Through these arrangements the Scottish Office may expect a regular flow of information on Community developments within its departmental responsibilities, Scottish Office officials will participate in the working parties of the Commission and working groups of the Council, and there will be occasions, largely limited to the Fisheries or Agriculture Councils, when a Scottish Office Minister will attend the Council as part of the United Kingdom delegation. In addition, there is usually one Scottish Office official seconded to UKREP, and the Scottish Office may benefit from informal information obtained through Scotland Europa in Brussels, although for policy reasons that body does not include any Scottish Office officials.

A Scottish Government will need to ensure that there are arrangements in place to provide it with a flow of information and an involvement in the Community legislative process in respect of its devolved competence at least comparable to that presently enjoyed by the Scottish Office. If these arrangements are left to be determined, post-devolution, the danger is that a Scottish Government will find itself at the end of a long and precarious line of communication. This would not necessarily be the result of any ill will, but obviously the position would be exacerbated if the political policies of a Scottish Government and the United Kingdom Government were divergent. In a careful analysis of this matter, the report of the Constitution Unit suggests that difficulties could be ameliorated if the Scottish Government were to establish its own office in Brussels and the civil servants in the Scottish Government were to remain part of the United Kingdom civil service.[12] These proposals raise their own difficulties. Although it may be desirable for a Scottish Government to have an office in Brussels for the purposes of garnering

---

[11] The report of the Constitution Unit (see note 8), at paras 343–348, notes these developments and suggests that there may be scope for a co-operation agreement between a Scottish Government and the United Kingdom Government relating to the participation of a Scottish Government in the Community legislative process, perhaps supported by a provision in devolution legislation requiring such an agreement.

[12] See note 8, paras 334, 429–438; cf Scottish Constitutional Convention, *Scotland's Parliament: Scotland's Right*, p 16.

information on Community developments and for lobbying, this would nevertheless be an informal arrangement; there should be within a devolution
scheme a clear obligation, preferably statutory, for the United Kingdom
Government to provide a Scottish Government with prompt information on
Community developments with direct and indirect effect on the competence of
a Scottish Government, and to consult the Scottish Government on such
developments. It will, after all, remain the responsibility of the United
Kingdom, as the member state, to negotiate Community policy and draft
legislation and take a position on them in the Council of Ministers. Maintaining
a unified United Kingdom civil service, at least initially after devolution, would
no doubt assist liaison on Community matters as well as others. However, this
also should be regulated by the devolution legislation, not least because it will
be important to have a clear understanding on whether a civil servant in the
Scottish Government is ultimately responsible to Her Majesty's Government in
Scotland or Her Majesty's Government in the United Kingdom.

A Scottish Parliament and the Community legislative process
Whatever arrangements were made for the involvement of the Scottish
Government in the Community legislative process, a Scottish Parliament
would expect to hold the Scottish Government to account for the manner in
which it exercised that role which, as indicated above, would be likely to be the
manner in which it pressed the United Kingdom Government over Scottish
concerns on draft Community legislation. To do this the Scottish Parliament
would probably find it necessary, as the House of Commons and House of
Lords did in 1974,[13] to establish a committee to scrutinise draft Community
legislation falling within its areas of legislative competence. Such a committee
would have a considerable task, which in turn would have resource implications.

One difficulty, which it would share with a Scottish Government, would be
ensuring an adequate flow of information on proposed and draft Community
legislation, and on proposed amendments to such legislation during the
Community legislative process. A way in which a Scottish Parliament and a
Scottish Government could ensure this would be for the Scottish Government
to give an undertaking to the Scottish Parliament that it would provide the
information on the same basis that the information is provided by the United

[13] See T. StJ. N. Bates, 'The Scrutiny of European Legislation at Westminster' 1 E L Rev
(1975–76) 22; Bates, 'The Scrutiny of Administration', in M. Ryle and P. G. Richards (eds), *The
Commons Under Scrutiny* (Routledge, 1988); Bates, 'Select Committees in the House of Lords',
in A. Drewry (ed), *The New Select Committees* (2nd edn, OUP, 1989). For recent consideration
of parliamentary scrutiny, see 27th Report, Select Committee on European Legislation, The
Scrutiny of European Business, H C 51-xxvii (1995–96).

Kingdom Government to Westminster. The United Kingdom Government undertaking to supply information to Westminster[14] was initially to provide a copy of each legislative proposal published by the Commission within forty-eight hours of the English version being received in Whitehall, and also an explanatory memorandum on the proposal within, in normal circumstances, two weeks thereafter. This undertaking has been extended and refined over the years to include, for example, information on substantial amendments to proposals when they are before the Council of Ministers and are of particular interest to the United Kingdom[15] and to inform Parliament of Commission proposals which have been withdrawn because of the degree of opposition within the Council. The undertaking also now extends to matters other than legislative proposals. Although these arrangements have not always worked well,[16] the undertakings do mean that Parliament can hold the Government responsible for a failure to provide the information. A similar undertaking to the Scottish Parliament by the Scottish Government should ensure that the Scottish Government, and consequently the Scottish Parliament, was provided with prompt and adequate information on Community developments. If it were politically feasible, it would be desirable to place the Scottish Government under a statutory obligation to provide such information to the Scottish Parliament, although admittedly the parallel Westminster arrangement does not have a statutory basis.

Either as an undertaking or as a statutory responsibility, this arrangement would appear to be preferable to other suggestions which have been mooted. One is that the Scottish Parliament should itself establish an office in Brussels to obtain information of Community developments.[17] This would be an essentially informal mechanism to obtain the information and, as an exclusive source of information, it appears to be a constitutionally inappropriate mechanism. An office could be established, but there appears to be no good reason why a Scottish Parliament should do so; neither the House of Lords nor the House of Commons has yet found it necessary to establish such an office.

Obtaining information would be only one of the operational difficulties which a committee established by the Scottish Parliament to scrutinise draft Community legislation would face. Another difficulty would be for the committee to synchronise its work with the Community legislative process. Nevertheless, despite such difficulties, if the terms of reference of such a

---

[14] 852 HC Debs, col 1115 *et seq*.

[15] 899 HC Debs, cols 36–38, 106–107.

[16] See, for example, First Special Report, Select Committee on European Legislation, HC 126–iv (1983–84).

[17] See Scottish Constitutional Convention, *Scotland's Parliament: Scotland's Right*, p 16; the Constitution Unit, *Scotland's Parliament: Fundamentals for a New Scotland Act*, para 333.

committee were to consider draft Community legislation falling within the competence of the Scottish Parliament and to report on such legislation that raised matters of serious political or legal concern for Scotland, the Scottish Parliament would be able to hold a Scottish Government to account for its role in the negotiation of such legislation in an informed way.

The question then arises whether a devolution scheme would give a Scottish Parliament any wider influence than this. At Westminster, the committees which scrutinise draft Community legislation have a somewhat enhanced status through the operation of what is sometimes called the parliamentary reserve. Where either the House of Lords or the House of Commons committee reports that a debate should be held on a draft Community legislative proposal, in most circumstances the Government will not agree to the legislation, or a common position on the legislation, in the Council of the European Union before the debate has taken place in Westminster.[18] In the Lords, debates on the reports of the scrutiny committee are held on the floor of the House. In the House of Commons the debate is, on the recommendation of the scrutiny committee, held either in one of the European Standing Committees or on the floor of the House. If the committee recommendation that debate takes place on the floor of the House is accepted by the Government, it is necessary for the Government to move a motion in the House to that effect, otherwise the Community documents recommended for debate are automatically referred to the appropriate European Standing Committee.[19] The creation of these standing committees in 1991 has meant that a much higher proportion of debates on draft Community legislation now take place off the floor of the House.

The procedure in these committees replicates the procedure in the special standing committees on public bills. A Minister from the department to which the draft Community legislation relates attends the committee and the committee may devote up to an hour in hearing the statement from the Minister and putting questions to him or her. After the statement and question period the Minister moves an amendable motion which is then debated. Each sitting of the committee on the draft Community legislation before it may last only two and a half hours, including the statement and question period. The chairman of the committee reports to the House any resolution of the committee, or that it has failed to come to a resolution. An amendable motion may be made thereafter in the House in respect of the committee report, but this motion is put without debate.

---

[18] See, for example, 178 HC Debs, col 339; 354 HL Debs, col 641.
[19] On the early work of the European Standing Committee, see T. StJ. N. Bates, 'European Community Legislation before the House of Commons' 12 Stat L R (1991) 109.

One study has suggested that a devolution scheme could include a parallel arrangement to this parliamentary reserve, where the Scottish Parliament resolved that draft Community legislation raised matters of political or legal concern for Scotland.[20] The report suggests that, subject to the same exceptions as apply at Westminster, where the Scottish Parliament had so resolved the United Kingdom Government could commit itself not to agree to the adoption of the Community legislation in the Council of Ministers until a debate had taken place on the substance of the Scottish Parliament's resolution at Westminster or the appropriate Westminster scrutiny committee had reported on the matter. At first blush this seems an attractive proposal, but it has constitutional and practical difficulties. Constitutionally, it seems inappropriate to reduce the Scottish Parliament to being essentially a privileged petitioner of Westminster. It would also probably prove impractical to accommodate these proposed arrangements within the Community legislative timetable; this has been a difficulty when only one domestic parliament is involved, it would be immeasurably greater if there were two involved.

In any event, it must be recognised that the parliamentary reserve mechanism has limitations as a means of ensuring parliamentary accountability for Government involvement in the Community legislative process. Under the present Westminster arrangements the United Kingdom Government can, for negotiating reasons, agree to the adoption of Community legislation on which there is an adverse Westminster committee report but no debate has taken place – although the reasons for doing so must be reported to Parliament. Of perhaps more significance, the Westminster procedure has a diminishing impact as the capacity of the Council of the European Union to adopt legislation by majority rather than unanimous vote increases.

Scottish legislation, a Scottish Government and Community obligations

The capacity of a Scottish Parliament to enact legislation, and of a Scottish Government to make delegated legislation or otherwise act within its statutory competence, would be subject to the Community legal obligations of the United Kingdom. A devolution scheme would include statutory mechanisms to ensure that neither the Scottish Parliament nor the Scottish Government exercised its devolved powers in breach of Community obligations, because it would be the United Kingdom Government that would attract responsibility for such a breach.

---

[20] Scotland's Parliament: Fundamentals for a New Scotland Act (The Constitution Unit, London, 1996), para 355.

The Scotland Act 1978 provided various mechanisms to address these matters. Section 19 placed the Secretary of State under a duty to consider every bill passed by the Scottish Assembly, and if he considered that any of its provisions were not within the legislative competence of the Assembly, or that there was sufficient doubt about the matter, he was under a duty to refer the question to the Judicial Committee of the Privy Council. One exception to this statutory duty was where the Secretary of State considered that a bill passed by the Assembly contained any provision which would, or might, affect a reserve matter either directly or indirectly and enacting the provision would not be in the public interest. In such a case he was empowered to lay the bill before the United Kingdom Parliament with a reasoned statement that, in his opinion, it ought not to be submitted for assent. If, within a period of twenty-eight days from the day on which it was laid each House resolved that the bill should not be submitted for assent, the bill would not be submitted.[21] Thus a Government view that primary legislation passed by the Scottish Assembly was not within its devolved legislative competence or affected a reserved matter was either referred for judicial determination or required the formal approval of both Houses of Parliament.

However, a different statutory power applied to primary legislation of the Scottish Assembly where Community obligations were in issue. Section 19(2) provided that: 'If … the Secretary of State is of opinion that the bill is not compatible with Community obligations … of the United Kingdom or that it provides for matters which are or ought to be provided for by or under legislation passed by Parliament and implementing any such obligation, he shall certify to the Assembly that he is of that opinion and shall not submit the bill to Her Majesty's Council for approval.' This provision applied to an Assembly bill which, in the view of the United Kingdom Government, was not compatible with its Community obligations but was otherwise within the legislative competence of the Assembly. Assent to such a bill was to be denied solely on the certificate of the Secretary of State to the Assembly. Section 19(1) specifically excluded referring such a bill to the Judicial Committee of the Privy Council for a decision on its compatibility with Community obligations. The best interpretation of s 19 also suggests that where the United Kingdom Government was of a view that an Assembly bill was both not compatible with the Community obligations of the United Kingdom and also outside the legislative competence of the Assembly, such a bill would not be submitted for assent solely on a certificate by the Secretary of State to the Assembly that he or she was of this opinion. Such a bill also seems to have been outwith the s 38

---

[21] Section 38.

procedure. Thus the opinion of the United Kingdom Government on what would appear to be entirely a question of law was excluded from judicial determination and was not even made the subject of a United Kingdom parliamentary procedure endorsing the opinion of the Government.

As far as subordinate legislation was concerned, s 40(2) empowered the Secretary of State to revoke by order an instrument made by the Scottish Executive, under any Act of Parliament or Scottish Assembly Act, if he considered it incompatible with the Community obligations of the United Kingdom or that it provided for any matter 'which is or ought to be provided for in an instrument made by the Secretary of State in implementing such an obligation'. Again, the opinion of the Secretary of State on a matter of law was not subject to judicial consideration, nor was an order revoking such subordinate legislation subject to any special United Kingdom parliamentary procedure.

This lack of a specific parliamentary procedure was in contrast to circumstances in which the Secretary of State revoked by order an instrument made by the Scottish Executive which he considered affected a reserved matter, directly or indirectly, and that the public interest made it desirable to exercise the power to revoke the instrument. In that case the order revoking the instrument required the approval of each House of Parliament before it was made or, in certain circumstances, if it were to continue to have effect.[22]

The s 40 powers related only to subordinate legislation which had been made, but not to such legislation which was in contemplation or which had been laid before the Assembly in draft and required its approval. It may be that in such circumstances the United Kingdom Government could have exercised its powers to direct the Scottish Executive either to act or desist from action where the action or inaction by the Scottish Executive was considered by the United Kingdom Government to be incompatible with Community obligations.[23] However, the exercise of that power was subject to the requirement for approval by each House of Parliament.[24]

In addition, the United Kingdom Government had a reserve power to implement a Community obligation by subordinate legislation where such subordinate legislation could be made by the Scottish Executive but the United Kingdom Government considered it desirable to make the subordinate legislation itself.[25]

---

[22] Section 40(5).
[23] Section 39(2).
[24] Section 39(6).
[25] Section 64(3).

The exclusion of the courts in the exercise of these powers under the 1978 Act was presumably motivated in part by the fact that once a question of compatibility of Assembly legislation or Scottish Executive delegated legislation with Community obligations was before a court there would be the prospect of the question being referred to the European Court of Justice for a preliminary ruling, with the possibility of the ruling having an indirect effect on domestic constitutional relationships, the potential for political embarrassment and the inevitable consequential delay. The extent to which the exercise of such powers could, or would, be excluded in the courts on these grounds today must be debatable.[26] There appears to be even less force in allowing the powers to be exercised without the requirement of any specified United Kingdom parliamentary procedure.

Furthermore, replicating these extensive powers of the United Kingdom Government in the 1978 Act would tend to erode the proper exercise of some of the functions of the Scottish Parliament. The Scottish Parliament might be expected to establish procedures for scrutinising the subordinate legislation made by the Scottish Government and such scrutiny would involve, for example, questions of whether the delegated legislation was in breach of Community law or failed to implement, or implement properly or fully, a Community directive. Similarly, it would be a function of the Scottish Parliament in the first instance to hold the Scottish Government to account for acting, failing to act or making subordinate legislation in breach of Community obligations.

A further point may be noted. If the powers of the United Kingdom Government in respect of bills passed by the Scottish Parliament or subordinate legislation made by the Scottish Government were to be made subject to judicial review, in whole or in part, this might well add another dimension to the debate on whether issues of legislative competence should be reviewed by the Judicial Committee of the Privy Council or the House of Lords. Where issues of Community law are involved, an argument may be made that the House of Lords, with a quarter of a century of experience of Community law, may be a preferable forum to the Judicial Committee augmented, as has been suggested in some quarters, by Commonwealth judges.

This does not exhaust the implications of replicating the s 19(2) and 40(2) powers of the United Kingdom Government with respect to primary legislation passed by a Scottish Parliament or made by a Scottish Executive. These powers under the 1978 Act could be exercised where the United Kingdom Government was not only of the opinion that the legislation was incompatible with

---

[26] Cf *R* v *Secretary of State for the Environment, ex p RSPB* [1995] JPL 842 (HL).

Community obligations but also in two other circumstances. The first was that the legislation provided for matters which were provided by primary legislation made by the United Kingdom Parliament or subordinate legislation made by the United Kingdom Government which implemented such obligation. Again, whether the United Kingdom legislation implemented the Community obligation would be a question of law and the arguments advanced above would be applicable here.

The powers could also be exercised where the United Kingdom Government considered that the Community obligation ought to be implemented by primary legislation of the United Kingdom Parliament or subordinate legislation of the United Kingdom Government, even where there was no doubt that the Scottish legislation was compatible with the Community obligation. Reaching such a view may reasonably be categorised as a matter of political judgment and arguably, therefore, a matter from which the courts should be excluded, although there would remain the question whether, in such circumstances, the devolved Scottish institutions could seek judicial review of whether the implementation by the United Kingdom Government or the United Kingdom Parliament satisfied the Community obligation. An argument that this power should not be subject to a specified United Kingdom parliamentary procedure seems less persuasive. There will obviously be circumstances in which the implementation of Community directives in the United Kingdom will best be undertaken entirely at Westminster or by Whitehall departments – for example, where the implementation involves both devolved and reserved areas of competence. However, an extensive exercise of such powers could have the effect of inhibiting the Scottish institutions from taking a distinctively Scottish position in implementing Community obligations. For example, if the Scottish Government and the Scottish Parliament decided to implement a Community directive in a manner distinct from that proposed in London, should this be a consideration which allows the United Kingdom Government to determine that the implementation of the directive should be exclusively undertaken by the United Kingdom Government and Parliament, excluding the Scottish Government and Parliament? It should at least be possible to test this question at Westminster.

The report of the Constitution Unit proposes a mechanism to ameliorate some of these difficulties. It states:

'A clause might be included in the legislation effectively to give the Scottish Parliament a period of grace of a year to implement [a Community] obligation for itself before Westminster intervenes. The clause, again making clear where liability for inaction lies, might be on the following lines: "(1) If Parliament legislates to give effect to an EC obligation in Scotland, in the absence of legislation of the Scottish Parliament giving full effect to that obligation as part of Scottish law, more than one year after the obligation has arisen, then any financial liability of the United Kingdom Government arising out of that failure is transferred to the Scottish Executive.""[27]

This may suggest a way forward, but the manner in which it is presently formulated has difficulties. They can best be shown by taking an example of implementing a Community directive. Directives contain a date by which member states must implement them. The Community legal obligation is to implement by that date. And, consequently, a statutory formulation referring to Westminster implementation 'more than one year after the obligation has arisen' is not meaningful. The proposed statutory wording also appears to suggest that the United Kingdom Government would not retain a mechanism under a devolution scheme to implement a Community obligation within an area of devolved legislative competence by United Kingdom primary or subordinate legislation. It seems unlikely that this would be the case, and if it retained such a power it would have the capacity to implement a Community obligation within matters of devolved legislative competence and consequently, in Community law, attract liability for failing to do so. If the United Kingdom retained such a power it is difficult to see why a Scottish Government should attract financial liability for the failure of the United Kingdom to exercise its powers to implement a Community obligation.

Scottish legislation and Community obligations
Finally, whatever procedures are put into place in a devolution scheme to protect the United Kingdom from being in breach of Community law as a consequence of legislation passed by a Scottish Parliament or made by a Scottish Executive, there is the prospect that such primary legislation will be enacted or subordinate legislation made and not revoked. The compatibility of such Scottish legislation with Community obligations may then come before domestic courts. The compatibility of the Scottish legislation with Community obligations is a question which, under art 177 of the EC Treaty, may, and in some circumstances must, be referred to the European Court of Justice for a preliminary ruling. It would also be possible for such questions of compatibility to arise in actions before the European Court of Justice itself.

[27] Paragraph 118.

Devolution and Regulatory Authorities

Robert Reed, QC

Introduction

For many years important functions have been entrusted in the public interest neither to central government nor to local government but to a wide variety of other agencies. It is impossible to state how many exist, as there is no agreed definition of the bodies concerned, but a reasonable estimate would be in excess of 1,000.[1] Their activities impinge on almost every aspect of life in Scotland, including those which the Scottish Constitutional Convention has proposed should fall within the ambit of a Scottish Parliament.[2] Their functions are diverse: some provide services (for example, the Post Office, the Bank of England, the BBC, National Health Service trusts); others distribute public funds (for example, the arts councils and the research councils); others again can be described as essentially 'regulatory'. The present discussion will focus on the latter category. Some examples may be given of bodies which can be described as 'regulatory':

(i) in relation to broadcasting, the Independent Television Commission[3] and the Radio Authority,[4] which license the independent television companies and local radio stations respectively; the Broadcasting Complaints Commission;[5] and the Broadcasting Standards Council;[6]

(ii) in respect of the police and the security services, Her Majesty's Inspectors of Constabulary,[7] the Interception Commissioner[8] and the Security Commission;[9]

---

[1] According to one official list, there were 1,444 non-departmental public bodies in the United Kingdom in 1991: Non-Departmental Public Bodies: A Guide for Departments (Cm 7797, 1991).

[2] Scotland's Parliament, Scotland's Right (Scottish Constitutional Convention, 1995).

[3] Broadcasting Act 1990, s 1.

[4] Ibid, s 83.

[5] Ibid, s 142.

[6] Ibid, s 151.

[7] Police (Scotland) Act 1967, s 33.

[8] Interception of Communications Act 1985, s 8.

[9] For an account, see I. Leigh and L. Lustgarten, 'The Security Commission: Constitutional Achievement or Curiosity?' [1991] PL 215.

(iii) in relation to air transport, the Civil Aviation Authority,[10] which licenses domestic air services and maintains safety standards;

(iv) the Commission for Racial Equality[11] and the Equal Opportunities Commission,[12] which enforce legislation against discrimination;

(v) the many bodies which regulate professions and occupations by means of licensing, registration and discipline, such as the Faculty of Advocates[13] and the General Medical Council;[14]

(vi) self-regulatory bodies created under government pressure or with government encouragement, such as the Press Complaints Commission[15] and the City Panel on Take-Overs and Mergers;[16] and

(vii) agencies established to regulate industries which were previously in public ownership, such as the Director General of Telecommunications (OFTEL),[17] the Director General of Gas Supply (OFGAS),[18] the Director General of Electricity Supply,[19] the Rail Regulator and the Director of Passenger Rail Franchising (OPRAF);[20] such agencies are often accompanied by other agencies representative of consumers – for example, the Gas Consumers Council[21] and Rail Users' Consultative Committees.[22]

As is apparent from the range of examples given, regulatory bodies vary greatly in their history, their legal structure and their legal status, as also in their relationships with Government and Parliament. Some are established by Royal Charter;[23] some are statutory corporations;[24] some are companies established under the Companies Acts;[25] some form part of the Crown;[26] some are unincorporated associations.[27] The extent to which, and means by which, they are subject to the control or influence of Parliament, the Government or

---

[10] Civil Aviation Act 1982, s 2, as amended.

[11] Race Relations Act 1976, s 43.

[12] Sex Discrimination Act 1975, s 53.

[13] See generally the *Stair Memorial Encyclopaedia*, vol. 1, paras 1302 ff; and, in relation to complaints, the Law Reform (Miscellaneous Provisions)(Scotland) Act 1990, s 33.

[14] Medical Act 1983, s 1; the General Medical Council (Constitution) Order 1979 (SI 1979/112), as amended.

[15] Established in 1991 following the Report of the Committee on Privacy and Related Matters (Cm 1102, 1990). See P. Milmo, 'The New Law of Privacy' (1993) 143 NLJ 1182.

[16] See *R v Panel of Takeovers and Mergers, ex parte Datafin plc* [1987] QB 815.

[17] Telecommunications Act 1984, s 1.

[18] Gas Act 1986, s 1.

[19] Electricity Act 1989, s 1.

[20] Railways Act 1993, s 1.

[21] Gas Act 1986, s 2.

[22] Railways Act 1993, s 2.

[23] For example, the Institute of Chartered Accountants of Scotland.

[24] For example, the Broadcasting Standards Council.

[25] For example, the Securities and Investments Board.

[26] For example, the Director of Passenger Rail Franchising probably falls into this category.

[27] For example, the Press Complaints Commission.

the courts vary widely. Typically, but not invariably, their members are appointed by a minister; they may or may not be subject to ministerial guidance in their activities; they may or may not be required to report to the minister; their reports may or may not have to be presented to Parliament. Generally, ministerial accountability to Parliament and its committees will reflect the extent to which the minister is responsible for the body's activities. Such bodies may or may not be subject to the jurisdiction of the Scottish courts, depending on their legal structure, legal status and location.[28]

In the context of proposals for the devolution of legislative and governmental functions from the Parliament and Government of the United Kingdom to Scottish institutions, regulatory authorities raise distinctive questions as to the extent to which, and means by which, they can or ought to be brought within the control or influence of a devolved Scottish Parliament or Scottish administration. The present discussion will not concern itself with the issues of economic or social policy, but will consider the constitutional and legal aspects.

The type of question which arises can be illustrated by an example. One of the subjects listed as a devolved matter in the Scotland Act 1978 was 'Provision of public passenger and freight transport services within Scotland. Payment of subsidies to operators of such services within Scotland'.[29]

Similarly, the Scottish Constitutional Convention has proposed as an area falling within the powers of Scotland's Parliament 'Transportation, including public passenger and freight services, and payment of subsidies to operators of such services'.[30]

Under the régime established by the Railways Act 1993, the award of contracts for the provision of passenger rail services in Scotland (and elsewhere in the United Kingdom) is the responsibility of the Franchising Director, who functions as an arm of the Secretary of State for Transport. He is reponsible for sums received and paid for the provision of passenger services under franchise agreements – that is, redistributing receipts from some franchisees in the form of subsidies to other operators. He has to specify the minimum service levels to be provided by operators. He is appointed by the Secretary of State, and can be removed (prior to the expiry of his appointment) only on the ground of incapacity or misbehaviour.[31] He has to fulfil, in accordance with instructions and guidance given to him by the Secretary of State, any objectives given to

---

[28] Cf *Bank of Scotland* v *Investment Management Regulatory Organisation Limited* 1989 SC 107. In practice, jurisdiction will normally be conceded by bodies acting under the aegis of the Government, even though the ground of jurisdiction may be debatable, as in *Highland Regional Council* v *Director of Passenger Rail Franchising* 1995 GWD 28-1509.

[29] Scotland Act 1978, Sched 10, Part 1, Group 10.

[30] See Scotland's Parliament, Scotland's Right, note 2 above, p 32.

[31] Railways Act 1993 s 1.

him by the Secretary of State.[32] Those objectives must be laid before Parliament,[33] whereas the instructions and guidance need not be (but have been). He consults with Rail Users' Consultative Committees, which consist of a chairman appointed by the Secretary of State and other members appointed by the Rail Regulator.[34] There is a consultative committee for Scotland.

When the Franchising Director published a consultation draft of the minimum service levels for the Scotrail franchise, concern was expressed in Scotland over the future of sleeper services between London and Fort William. This culminated in an application for judicial review.[35] The concern was not restricted to the level of service within Scotland: it related to the level of service between London and Carlisle as much as to that between Carlisle and Fort William. Moreover, since the Franchising Director is required to operate a budget which is fixed for Great Britain as a whole, his decision as to the level of subsidy appropriate for a service which was socially important in Scotland would also have implications for services in England and Wales. His decision was thus of legitimate interest not only in Scotland but also in England and Wales.

In the context of devolution, accordingly, one could not expect the existing powers and duties of the Secretary of State for Transport in relation to the Franchising Director simply to be transferred to a Scottish administration, even if the transferred responsibilities were restricted to matters concerning passenger rail services in Scotland. Any such transfer of powers and duties would necessitate changes to the structure and responsibilities of the office of the Franchising Director, including financial responsibilities (for example, to 'ring-fence' receipts and payments in respect of services provided by franchisees in Scotland), and would have to reflect the nature of any such changes. Such an exercise would plainly involve issues of economic and social policy, as to which the views of the United Kingdom Government and Parliament on the one hand, and the Scottish administration and Parliament on the other hand, might not coincide.

As will appear, issues raised by regulatory authorities in the context of devolution have not been considered in detail by the Scottish Constitutional Convention. They were however addressed in the Scotland Act 1978.

The Scotland Act 1978

The approach adopted in the Scotland Act 1978 in relation to regulatory authorities had the effect of dividing them into three categories.

[32] Ibid, s 5(1).
[33] Ibid, s 5(3).
[34] Ibid, s 2.
[35] *Highland Regional Council* v *Director of Passenger Rail Franchising* 1995 GWD 28–1509.

In the first place, the Act made no provision in respect of bodies whose remit related solely to reserved matters. This reflected the basic scheme of the Act, whereby only specified powers were devolved to the Scottish Assembly and Scottish Executive. Bodies which were concerned solely with reserved matters were therefore unaffected by the Act, and no specific provision required to be made for them.

In relation to bodies concerned with devolved matters, the position was more complex. Schedule 10 described matters falling within the legislative competence of the Scottish Assembly and within the powers of the Scottish Executive. Schedule 11 described certain additional matters falling within the powers of the Scottish Executive but *not* within the legislative competence of the Scottish Assembly. In principle, where a body's remit concerned matters falling within Sched 10, legislative competence (so far as extending to Scotland) in respect of that body was transferred from the United Kingdom Parliament to the Scottish Assembly (by s 18 and Sched 2), and existing executive powers, and powers to make subordinate legislation, held by a minister of the Crown were transferred to a Scottish Secretary (by ss 21, 22 and 63). In addition, certain statutory powers listed in Sched 11 were also vested in a Scottish Secretary.

The general approach described in the previous paragraph was subject to a number of qualifications, of which one was of particular importance. Schedule 13 to the Act specified a number of bodies which were responsible for reserved as well as devolved matters and/or which operated in England and Wales as well as in Scotland. Examples were the British Airports Authority and the Civil Aviation Authority. Section 69 excluded bodies listed in Sched 13 from the scope of ss 21 and 22. Accordingly, ministerial powers in respect of such bodies were not transferred by those sections to a Scottish Secretary. Similarly, by virtue of para 5 of Sched 2, provisions relating to such bodies were not automatically within the competence of the Scottish Assembly. Section 69, however, empowered a minister to make an order transferring some or all ministerial powers or duties in respect of such a body to a Scottish Secretary.[36] Such powers might, for example, include the power to make some of the appointments to the body, or to issue directions on the activities of the body in question. The powers might be transferred absolutely, or on the basis that they be exercised by a Scottish Secretary with the consent of a minister of the Crown.[37] In making an order under s 69, the minister could alter the existing constitution of the body – for example, by requiring or authorising the appointment of additional members, or apportioning any assets or liabilities, or

[36] Scotland Act 1978, s 69(2)(a).
[37] Ibid.

imposing (or enabling the imposition of) any limits in addition to or in substitution for existing limits.[38] The order could provide for a division of financial responsibility, so that the 'devolved' activities of the body in question would be financed from the Scottish Consolidated and Loans Funds, and so that the accounts of the body's activities financed from those funds were submitted to the Scottish Assembly rather than to Parliament.[39] Generally, the order could contain 'such provisions … as appear to the Minister … necessary or expedient in consequence of other provisions of the order or incidental or supplementary thereto'.[40] An order could be made under s 69 only at the request of a Scottish Secretary,[41] and only after consultation with the body concerned.[42] The making of an order was however at the discretion of the minister;[43] and it could be made only with the approval of both Houses of Parliament.[44] Once an order was made, the restriction imposed upon the legislative competence of the Scottish Assembly was removed.[45]

Section 69 thus provided machinery for achieving a division of responsibility in respect of the bodies to which it applied. The basic effect of the section was to enable the United Kingdom Government to make adjustments to the structure, powers and duties of the bodies in question and to devolve ministerial responsibilities in respect of such bodies to the Scottish administration. Until an order was made, such bodies would continue to operate as they had previously done. Once an order was made in respect of such a body, it would be competent for the Scottish Assembly to legislate in respect of that body, provided of course that the matter to which the legislation related was a devolved matter. Thus, for example, if the minister made an order conferring powers or duties in respect of such a body on a Scottish Secretary, it would be possible for the Assembly to alter them, so far as relating to a devolved matter.

The Scottish Constitutional Convention

The basic scheme proposed by the Scottish Constitutional Convention is the same as that contained in the 1978 Act, namely that a distinction should be drawn between matters in respect of which sole legislative competence is

---

[38] Ibid, s 69(2)(b)–(d).

[39] Ibid, s 69(2)(e)–(g).

[40] Ibid, s 69(2).

[41] Ibid, s 69(3). There was an exception in respect of the Housing Corporation, on the assumption that the Scottish administration would require such an order to be made so as to implement its devolved responsibility in relation to housing.

[42] Ibid, s 69(3).

[43] Ibid, s 69(1).

[44] Ibid, s 69(4).

[45] Ibid, Sched 2, para 5.

retained by the United Kingdom Parliament, and matters in respect of which legislative competence is conferred on the Scottish Parliament. The Scottish Parliament's powers are to be set out in an Act of Parliament, and a list of the principal areas in question is provided in the Convention's report.[46] Although the list is more widely drawn (and less precisely defined) than in the 1978 Act,[47] the legislative approach is technically identical. Regulatory bodies operate in most, if not all, of the areas listed. The report acknowledges in general terms the existence of non-elected governmental bodies, and envisages that the Scottish Parliament will possess 'power to examine the role of quangos operating in Scotland, and to bring their activities under democratic control where it considers this necessary. It will also have powers to ensure that where such bodies remain they will be subject to greater accountability and accessibility'.[48]

Merger control

The report does not attempt a detailed consideration of regulatory authorities, and specific proposals are made in respect of only a few areas. One concerns 'mergers, competition policy and monopolies', which is not listed as a devolved matter. The report envisages[49] the continuing existence of the Monopolies and Mergers Commission, with a power of reference in respect of mergers conferred on the Scottish Parliament analogous to that presently possessed by the Secretary of State. The report does not set out the reasons for this proposal.

The power to refer mergers to the Monopolies and Mergers Commission is presently conferred on 'the Secretary of State',[50] an expression which in principle includes any of Her Majesty's Principal Secretaries of State.[51] In practice, the relevant powers are exercised by the President of the Board of Trade. No powers in relation to mergers are held specifically by the Secretary of State for Scotland, although he may have an involvement (along with the President of the Board of Trade) in references in respect of monopolies.[52]

The proposal to empower the Scottish Parliament to make merger references would thus necessitate the amendment of the Fair Trading Act 1973 by the United Kingdom Parliament. A number of issues would arise. One issue would be whether the conferment of a power of reference upon the Scottish

---

[46] See Scotland's Parliament, Scotland's Right, note 2 above, p 32.
[47] Scotland Act 1978, Sched 10.
[48] See Scotland's Parliament, Scotland's Right, note 2 above, p 17.
[49] Ibid, p 13.
[50] Fair Trading Act 1973, ss 59, 64 and 75.
[51] Interpretation Act 1978, Sched 1. It is arguable that in the context of the Fair Trading Act 1973 the expression refers specifically to the Secretary of State for Trade: see s 51(1) and (3).
[52] Fair Trading Act 1973, s 51.

Parliament was consistent with the treatment of mergers, competition policy
and monopolies as a reserved matter. At first sight, the proposal is very difficult
to reconcile with the general approach of treating mergers, competition policy
and monopolies as a reserved matter; and it is also debatable whether, if this
area is to be devolved to some extent, mergers in particular should be singled
out.[53] A second issue would be whether it would be appropriate to confer a
power of reference upon the Scottish Parliament rather than upon a member
of the Scottish administration, such as one of its ministers.[54] This depends in
part upon the nature of the Parliament: whether it is a representative body to
which the elected Government is answerable for its executive actions (along
the lines of the Westminster Parliament), or whether it is a body which
(directly, or through its committees) takes executive action. Merger references
are executive actions which often require to be taken urgently and on the basis
of information which cannot be made public; and it might be questioned
whether such actions could appropriately be left in the hands of a parliamentary body. A third issue would concern the appropriate relationship between
any power of reference conferred on the Scottish Parliament, the power to vary
references (presently held by the President of the Board of Trade),[55] powers to
make interim orders,[56] the subsequent report by the Monopolies and Mergers
Commission (presently submitted to the President of the Board of Trade),[57]
the laying of the report before Parliament[58] and the ultimate decision
(presently a matter for the President of the Board of Trade).[59] Consideration
would also have to be given to the implications of such a power for numerous

---

[53] Mergers can be politically sensitive where they result in the control of Scottish companies or
   their headquarters going outwith Scotland (as, for example, in the Guinness takeover of
   Distillers); but competition and monopolies can have consequences which are of equal
   economic or social significance, although they may be less dramatic. Subjecting Scottish
   businesses to a level of scrutiny and control additional to those operating south of the border
   may also have unintended effects on business location. And how is a Scottish business to be
   defined so as to bring it effectively within the ambit of the proposed merger control? Possible
   options would include the location of a company's registered office, or the location of its central
   management and control. The former can be readily defined and ascertained, and cannot be
   relocated outwith Scotland without a private Act of Parliament; but it need not correspond to
   the location of the company's central management and control, or indeed to any of its day-to-day
   operations, and to that extent it is a somewhat arbitrary test. A test based on the location of a
   company's central management and control, on the other hand, would give rise to practical
   difficulties in its application. Such problems could be avoided if the Scottish Parliament's power
   of reference was general in scope rather than being confined to Scottish businesses (however
   defined); but an unrestricted power of reference might not be politically acceptable.
[54] See Scotland's Parliament, Scotland's Right, note 2 above, p 25.
[55] Fair Trading Act 1973, s 71.
[56] Ibid, ss 74 and 89.
[57] Ibid, ss 59(3) and 64.
[58] Ibid, s 83.
[59] Ibid, ss 58 and 73.

other aspects of the current legislation (for example, as to the powers and duties of the Director General for Fair Trading,[60] the basis on which the public interest is to be assessed by the Commission,[61] and powers of appointment to the Commission and to the office of Director). In short, before the proposal of the Scottish Constitutional Convention could be implemented, or even fully considered, it would be essential to give detailed consideration to an appropriate division of responsibilities and an appropriate institutional framework. This would be a highly complex exercise requiring an assessment of legal, political, economic and administrative issues.

More fundamentally, competition policy in general and merger control in particular have to be addressed in the context of developments in European law and practice. The trend is towards regulation on a Europe-wide basis, using the Single Market as a reference point and adopting the integration of that market as an objective.[62] In that context, the future operation of controls based on national social and industrial policies is likely to be problematical, as is the use of a national market as a point of reference. At the same time, there is also a movement towards the decentralised enforcement of competition law, not least by private action before national courts.[63] This raises a variety of legal problems which will require to be resolved (for example, in respect of access to information held by Government or private bodies, confidentiality and the protection of business secrets, the legal duties involved in competition matters, issues of causation, and the assessment of damages). Issues of this kind will require to be considered by Scottish institutions responsible for the decentralised enforcement of a supranational system of competition law.

Broadcasting
A second area discussed is broadcasting, which is envisaged as being a devolved matter. The report proposes that

> 'The Parliament will initially assume responsibility for the existing role of the Secretary of State for Scotland in relation to broadcasting and the media in Scotland and will be able to promote broadcasting in Scotland, and ensure that it remains sensitive to Scottish needs. To keep pace with developments in Scotland, the UK and internationally, these roles will develop within the UK regulatory framework and must be kept under review.'[64]

Before commenting on this proposal, it may be helpful to give an outline of

---

[60] See, eg, ibid, s 88.
[61] Ibid, s 84.
[62] See, eg, the Merger Regulation, Reg EEC/4064/89.
[63] See *Automec* v *Commission* [1992] 5 CMLR 431; Hoskins, 'Garden Cottage Revisited: The Availability of Damages in the National Courts for Breaches of EEC Competition Rules' [1992] 6 ECLR 257.
[64] See Scotland's Parliament, Scotland's Right, note 2 above, p 15.

the existing regulatory framework. The BBC is regulated in the first place by its Charter[65] and by its Licence Agreement[66] negotiated by the Secretary of State for National Heritage. It also has statutory duties relating to the inclusion of independent productions in its television services.[67] It is also subject to the jurisdiction of the Broadcasting Complaints Commission[68] and the Broadcasting Standards Council.[69] The only direct Government control which can be exercised over BBC services is under art 13(4) of the licence, which entitles the Home Secretary (whose functions in this respect have been taken over by the Secretary of State for National Heritage) to require the BBC to refrain from broadcasting any specified matter.[70] Television programme services provided from places within the United Kingdom (other than BBC services) and local delivery services (that is, cable services within the United Kingdom) are regulated by the Independent Television Commission.[71] The only direct Government control is under s 10 of the Broadcasting Act 1990, which empowers the Secretary of State or any other minister of the Crown to require the Commission to direct licence-holders to broadcast an announcement or to refrain from broadcasting any specified matter.[72]

Satellite television services transmitted from within the United Kingdom fall within the jurisdiction of the Independent Television Commission. Foreign satellite services are generally outside the jurisdiction of the Commission and the Radio Authority, but can be proscribed by the Secretary of State if he is notified by the Commission or the Radio Authority that they are unacceptable and if he is satisfied that the proscribing of the service is compatible with the United Kingdom's international obligations.[73] Cable services within the United Kingdom are regulated by the Commission.[74] Independent radio services are regulated by the Radio Authority.[75] The only direct Government control is under s 94 of the 1990 Act, which empowers the Secretary of State or any other minister of the Crown to require the Radio Authority to direct licence-holders to broadcast a specified announcement. Complaints arising from television

---

[65] See Cmnd 8313, as amended; Cmnd 9013 (1983).

[66] Cmnd 8233.

[67] Broadcasting Act 1990, s 186.

[68] Ibid, s 143(2).

[69] Ibid, s 152(3).

[70] For an example, see *R v Secretary of State for the Home Department, ex parte Brind* [1991] 1 AC 696.

[71] Broadcasting Act 1990, s 2.

[72] For an example, see *ex parte Brind*, note 70 above.

[73] Broadcasting Act 1990, ss 177 and 178. The principal international obligation is contained in EEC Directive 89/552. For an example, see *R v Secretary of State for the National Heritage, ex parte Continental Television* [1993] EMLR 389.

[74] Broadcasting Act 1990, s 73.

[75] Ibid, s 84.

broadcasts can be considered and adjudicated upon by the Broadcasting Complaints Commission.[76] A more general supervisory power is exercised by the Broadcasting Standards Council.[77] The Government has indicated its intention to amalgamate the Broadcasting Complaints Commission and the Broadcasting Standards Council into a single body.[78]

It will be evident from the foregoing summary that the Government's direct involvement in the regulation of broadcasting is very limited. Apart from the various powers to require announcements to be broadcast (or to direct that specified matter *not* be broadcast), the only direct function relates to offensive satellite broadcasts from outwith the United Kingdom, which function is exercised by the Secretary of State for National Heritage in accordance with European law. Regulatory functions are exercised almost entirely by regulatory agencies, the members of which are appointed by the Secretary of State for National Heritage. The Secretary of State for National Heritage can also influence the Independent Television Commission by, for example, listing events (the FA Cup Final, the SFA Cup Final, the Grand National, etc) which should not be broadcast on a pay-per-view basis.[79] The Secretary of State for National Heritage is in a position to exercise some indirect influence over the BBC also in consequence of its dependence on the Government-controlled licence fee.

Considering the proposals of the Scottish Constitutional Convention in the context described above, it is difficult to reconcile the treatment of broadcasting as a devolved matter with the retention of the existing United Kingdom regulatory framework, which (so far as it is controlled by the Government) is under the control of the Secretary of State for National Heritage and is regulated by bodies which report to the United Kingdom Parliament. Some sort of formal division of responsibility between the Secretary of State and the United Kingdom Parliament, on the one hand, and the Scottish minister and the Scottish Parliament on the other hand, with consequent alterations to the constitutions and responsibilities of the regulatory bodies, would be essential if a meaningful devolution of functions in respect of broadcasting were to be achieved.

Any such division would also have to reflect the technological, commercial and legal problems which would be involved in regulating broadcasting on a Scottish basis. Satellite broadcasting operates on a technological and legal basis

---

[76] Ibid, s 143. For an example, see *R v Broadcasting Complaints Commission, ex parte Owen* [1985] QB 1153.

[77] Broadcasting Act 1990, s 152.

[78] Cm 2621.

[79] Broadcasting Act 1990, s 182.

which transcends national boundaries: its continent-wide 'footprints' have resulted in the regulation of its activities on an international basis, and have also conferred upon it a commercial power which can exceed that of national terrestrial broadcasters such as the BBC. If the intention behind the Convention's proposals is to protect and encourage Scottish culture (such as sport, religion, education, politics and law), it may be difficult to impose that objective on satellite broadcasters; apart from some sport and news, the culture of Scotland is bound to be of limited significance when the intended audience extends far beyond the borders of Scotland. The BBC, on the other hand, is required by its Charter to take Scottish culture and institutions into account; but the future of public service broadcasting, in the face of competition from satellite and cable services, depends on commercial and technological developments which cannot be regulated by law.

These observations are not intended as criticism of the Convention's report. The report is a political document expressing objectives of a general nature, rather than a set of instructions to parliamentary counsel: as it expressly recognises, detailed work of a legal nature remains to be done.[80]

A framework for legislation

In dealing with regulatory authorities, legislation creating a devolved system of government can be drafted without undue complexity, and be made workable, if it is based upon two fundamental principles, both of which were adopted in the Scotland Act 1978 and remain consistent with the aims of the Scottish Constitutional Convention:

(i) the devolution legislation should not itself alter the structure, powers, duties etc. of such bodies, but should provide a framework whereby such alterations can be effected in the future where appropriate. The devolution legislation should itself take such bodies as they presently stand;
(ii) the devolution legislation should distinguish between three categories of regulatory body:
    (a) those whose remit relates solely to reserved matters;
    (b) those whose remit relates solely to devolved matters, and which operate wholly within Scotland; and
    (c) the remainder.

Category (a) bodies are not legally affected by devolution. Since the devolution legislation does not concern itself with functions retained by the

---

[80] See *Scotland's Parliament, Scotland's Right*, note 2 above, p 30.

United Kingdom Government and Parliament, it can ignore category (a) bodies.

Category (b) bodies are at the other extreme: they are bodies in respect of which the United Kingdom Government and Parliament need not retain any function. Legislative power in respect of such bodies should therefore be devolved to the Scottish Parliament, and existing governmental powers should be transferred to the Scottish administration. Appropriate provisions for achieving these purposes can be found in the 1978 Act.[81]

Category (c) bodies are ones which transcend boundaries, which may be functional or geographical, or both. They may be concerned with functions which, within Scotland, are devolved, but which extend beyond Scotland (for example, passenger rail services); or they may be concerned within Scotland with functions some of which are devolved but others of which are retained by the United Kingdom Government and Parliament (the Civil Aviation Authority or the broadcasting regulatory agencies might be examples of such bodies). The obvious way of dealing with category (c) bodies in the context of devolution is to achieve a division of responsibilities between the United Kingdom Parliament and the Scottish Parliament, and between the United Kingdom Government and the Scottish administration. The division would be based upon functional boundaries, or upon territorial boundaries, as appropriate. It might include provisions as to the appointment of members, or as to reporting obligations, or as to financial matters (to give only a few examples), depending on the nature of the particular body in question. Such provisions would entail altering the existing legal structure of the body in question, and would have to be tailored to the particular case. Accordingly, the devolution legislation should not itself attempt to achieve the division of responsibilities in respect of category (c) bodies; rather, it should provide machinery whereby such a division could be effected in the future. A model of such machinery is to be found in s 69 of the 1978 Act, albeit in certain respects[82] it may not reflect some current aspirations.

Ministerial, parliamentary and judicial controls

The foregoing discussion has been concerned with the techniques which might be adopted in drafting devolution legislation. It remains to consider briefly the implications for ministerial, parliamentary and judicial control of regulatory authorities.

---

[81] In particular, ss 18, 21, 22 and 63.

[82] For example, whether orders should be capable of being revoked by other orders; or the extent to which the machinery should be under the control of each of the institutions involved.

Category (a) bodies

If devolution legislation were to follow the framework discussed above, the status quo would be maintained in respect of category (a) bodies. They would be subject to ministerial and parliamentary control only at United Kingdom level, and would be subject to judicial control to the same extent as at present.

Category (b) bodies

In relation to category (b) bodies, the Scottish administration would initially exercise the same controls as were previously exercised by the United Kingdom Government. This situation could be altered in the future by legislation passed by the Scottish Parliament. The Scottish Parliament would itself exercise such controls as it developed through its procedures and structures. These might or might not correspond to those previously exercised at Westminster (for example, through parliamentary questions, debates and select committees). Judicial controls would not be altered by devolution, but could be affected by future legislation promulgated by a Scottish Parliament or administration.

Category (c) bodies

In relation to category (c) bodies, the status quo would be maintained until the machinery for achieving a division of responsibilities was activated. The nature and extent of any controls exercised by the Scottish administration, the Scottish Parliament and the Scottish courts would depend upon the details of any scheme of division.

The Authors

William Bain holds an LLB degree and a Diploma in Legal Practice from the University of Strathclyde. He is a tutor in law at that university, specialising in local government law, administrative law and constitutional law.

St John Bates was appointed Clerk of Tynwald, Secretary of the House of Keys and Counsel to the Speaker in 1987. Previously he taught public law principally in Scotland, first at the University of Edinburgh, at which time he also acted as a specialist adviser to the House of Lords Select Committee on the European Communities, and later as John Millar Professor of Law at the University of Glasgow. Following his appointment in the Isle of Man he has continued a part-time academic career, successively holding appointments as Professor of Law at the University of Lancaster, as a Fellow of Wolfson College, Cambridge, and now as Professor of Law and Director of the Centre for Parliamentary and Legislative Studies at the University of Strathclyde. Since 1989 he has been the editor of the *Statute Law Review*.

Colin Boyd, QC, studied politics and economics at Manchester University and law at the University of Edinburgh. He practised as a solicitor before being admitted to the Scottish Bar in 1983. He is a Legal Associate of the Royal Town Planning Institute. He was an Advocate-Depute from 1993 to 1995 and took silk in the latter year.

Charles Haggerty holds an LLB(Hons) degree and a Diploma in Legal Practice from the University of Strathclyde, and has also undertaken study at the University of Leiden in the Netherlands. Currently he is a graduate teaching assistant at the University of Strathclyde, teaching Public Law and Law and the Legal Process, and a member of the Centre for Parliamentary and Legislative Studies, University of Strathclyde. His research interests include constitutional law, devolution, emergency powers, and human rights and civil liberties. He is currently researching for an LLM in the area of comparative emergency powers.

Gordon Jackson, QC, holds the degree of LLB from the University of St Andrews. After practice as a solicitor he was admitted to the Scottish Bar in 1979. He was an Advocate-Depute from 1979 to 1990. Called to the English

Bar in 1986, he took silk in 1990. He specialises in litigation, particularly in the criminal court.

Jean McFadden, CBE, JP, has the degrees of MA in Classics from the University of Glasgow and LLB from the University of Strathclyde. She is a lecturer in Public Law at the University of Strathclyde. She has been an elected member of the City Council in Glasgow since 1971 and served as a local government representative on the Executive Committee on the Scottish Constitutional Convention from its inception until 1996.

Robert Reed, QC, was admitted to the Scottish Bar in 1983 and was appointed Queen's Counsel in 1995. He was Standing Junior Counsel to the Scottish Office Home and Health Department between 1988 and 1995, and is currently an Advocate-Depute. He specialises in administrative and European law.